Erb by William Pett Ridge

William Pett Ridge was born at Chartham, near Canterbury, Kent on 22nd April 1859.

His family's resources were certainly limited. His father was a railway porter, and his son, after schooling in Marden, Kent became a clerk in a railway clearing house. The hours were long and arduous, but self improvement was his goal. After working from nine until seven o'clock he attended evening classes at Birkbeck Literary and Scientific Institute and then he would write.

From 1891 his humourous sketches were published in the St James's Gazette, the Idler, Windsor Magazine and other literary periodicals of the day. He was heavily influenced by Dickens and critics thought he might be his successor.

Pett Ridge published his first novel in 1895, A Clever Wife. By his fifth novel, Mord Em'ly, three years later, his success was obvious. His writing was written from the perspective of those born with no privilege and relied on talent to find humour and sympathy in his portrayal of working class life.

Today Pett Ridge and other East End novelists including Arthur Nevinson, Arthur Morrison & Edwin Pugh are grouped together as the Cockney Novelists.

With his success Pett Ridge gave generously of both time and money to charity. In 1907 he founded the Babies Home at Hoxton, one of several children's organisations

His circle considered Pett Ridge to be one of life's natural bachelors. In 1909 they were rather surprised therefore when he married Olga Hentschel.

As the 1920's arrived Pett Ridge added to his popularity with the movies. Four of his books were adapted into films.

Pett Ridge now found the peak of his fame had passed. He still managed to produce a book a year but was falling out of fashion and favour with the reading public. His canon runs to over sixty novels and short story collections as well as many pieces for magazines and periodicals.

William Pett Ridge died, on 29th September 1930, at his home, Ampthill, Willow Grove, Chislehurst, at the age of 71.

Index of Contents
"ERB"
CHAPTER I
CHAPTER II
CHAPTER III
CHAPTER IV
CHAPTER V
CHAPTER VI
CHAPTER VII

CHAPTER VIII
CHAPTER IX
CHAPTER X
CHAPTER XI
CHAPTER XII
CHAPTER XIII
CHAPTER XIV
CHAPTER XV
CHAPTER XVI
CHAPTER XVII
WILIAM PETT RIDGE – A SHORT BIOGRAPHY
WILLIAM PETT RIDGE – A CONCISE BIBLIOGRAPHY

CHAPTER I

"But I am reminded," shouted the scarlet faced man on the chair, still keeping his voice to the high note on which he had started, "I am reminded that my time is exhausted. Another talented speaker is 'ere to address you. I refer to our friend Barnes—better known per'aps to all of you as Erb."

The crescent shaped crowd, growling applause, gave signs of movement, and a round faced young man, standing at the side of the chair, looked up modestly at the sky.

"He, as you all know, 'ails from the district of Berminsey, where he exercises a certain amount of influence, and, in spite of his youth, is recognised as a positive power in the labour world. He is accustomed to hit straight from the shoulder, and he fears neether friend nor foe. I am going to tell you some'ing you very like don't know, and there's no necessity for it to go any further; that is that he stands a vurry good chance of being made the secretary of a new society. Friends! without further remarks from me, I call upon Comrade Barnes, better known as Erb, to address you. Thanks."

The man stepped down from the chair. "Where's my hat been and gone?" he asked. "Someone's shifted it."

The hour being half past twelve, the crowd had no business of an urgent nature for thirty minutes. A few strolled away to join other groups, and Herbert Barnes, as he took off his bowler hat and stepped upon the green chair, watched these sternly. Southwark Park was being wooed by the morning sun of spring time, the green fresh grass covered a space that was here and there protected by warning boards; the trees, after a shivering winter, were clothing themselves with a suit of new leaves. Away to the right, masts of shipping in the Surrey Commercial Docks showed high and gaunt above the middle aged trees that fringed the park: on the other side rows of small houses pressed closely. A few light haired Scandinavian sailors looked on amiably; timber carrying men, who showed a horny skin at the back of their necks, as badges of their labour, made up, with railway men in unaccustomed mufti, the rest of the group. The new speaker's features relaxed slightly as he saw two girls, conspicuous in the presence of so many men, join his audience, to resume his earlier manner when one exclaimed disappointedly, "Oh, it's only joring!" and both strolled away towards a bed of flaming tulips. A tall young woman, slightly lame, took their place.

"Friends," said Erb, very quietly, "I was not altogether prepared to be called upon for an address this morning, but—All right, my lad," this in reply to an appeal from the outside of the crescent, "I'll speak up presently. I'll speak up when I'm ready, in a way that'll make even you understand me." The line of speakers near the chair smiled, and the interjector's friends remarked gleefully that this was one in the eye for him. "I say that I came 'ere to this park this morning," he went on, raising his voice defiantly, and smoothing his obstinate hair with one hand, "more as a listener than a teacher, more ready to learn from others than to learn them anything myself." The tall young person on the edge of the crowd winced. "But as I have been called upon, I shall take the liberty of askin' you one or two very straight questions. My friend from Camberwell, who preceded, referred to me as one accustomed to hit straight from the shoulder; that's the way I'm going to play the game this morning. I stand up 'ere," he said, commencing to finger the buttons of his waistcoat, "as a working man addressing his fellow working men. Prouder titles there can never be, and if they was to offer to make me Lord Mayor of London at this present moment I should make answer to the effect that I preferred to be a working man." A voice on the outside asked where he worked? "I am a parcels carman on a railway I am, and I earn twenty three shillings and sixpence a week." A voice said it was a shame to pay a van boy the money earned by grown men; Herbert Barnes flushed at this and went on. The voice, deluded, threw at him another remark. "Was he" (asked the voice), "was he a half timer?"

"I'm going to spare one minute with this chap," said Erb, turning suddenly. "Bring him forward! Stand back from him then, if he's too shy for that, and let's see who we're dealing with. Oh, it's you, is it?"

"Yus," admitted the owner of the voice resentfully, "it is me."

"You don't look 'appy," said Erb.

"I've been listening to you," explained the man.

"Take your 'ands out of your pockets and let's 'ave a look at them." The man turned to go, but the circle declined to permit this. "Take a sight at his little hansy pansy." Order complied with. "What d'you make of 'em?" "Soft," retorted the expert. "I knew he was a loafer," said Erb. "Let him go now and prop up his favourite pubs; I want to talk to genuine working men, not to bits of touch wood. My first question is," here he referred to the notes on the back of an envelope which he held in his hand, "my first question is, what is it we working men most keenly desire at the present moment?"

"Tankard of bitter," said someone.

"Ah!" Herbert Barnes whirled round, and pointed a forefinger at the humorist and his friends. "There's a man who speaks the truth. There's a man what says jest the thing he really thinks. There's a man who utters that which is uppermost in his mind. There's a man," he leaned forward as though about to give one last applauding compliment, "whose 'ighest ambition, whose most elevated thought, whose one supreme anxiety is for a tankard of bitter. Friends," with a whirl of both arms, "we talk about the tyranny and what not of capital; the enmity of the upper circles, but there, jest over there, is the class of man that is our greatest opponent, the man from whom we have most to fear. A ten kard of bit ter!" he repeated deliberately.

"Well, but," said the humorist in an injured tone, "I suppose a chep can open his mouth?"

"You can open your mouth, and when you do, apparently, it's generally for the purpose of em'tying down it a—"

He hesitated. The crowd, glad to find personalities introduced, gave the words in a muffled chorus.

"Makin' a bloomin' song of it," grumbled the humorist, going off. "Some people can't take a joke."

"'Aving finished with our friend," said Herbert Barnes, loudly, "we will now resume our attention to our original argument. What is it that the working man—"

His voice grew so much in volume that people at Christadelphian and other crowds near the iron gates deserted these, and came across in the hope of better sport. One of his arguments created some dissension, and two men, detaching themselves from the crescent, went off to debate it, and an interested circle formed around these, listening with almost pained interest, and seemingly (from the nodding of their heads) convinced by each argument in turn. The round faced young man on the Windsor chair, now aiming the fist of one hand into the palm of the other as he laboured at an argument, and giving a tremendous and convincing thump as he made his point, noted the new crowd with approval: it was good to have said the stimulating thing. There were no interrupters now, but occasionally a voice would throw an approving sentence, caught neatly by Herbert Barnes, and used if he thought it wise or necessary; his best retorts were given with a glance at the one young woman of the crowd. He was in the middle of a long sentence decked out with many a paraphrase, and whole regiments of adjectives hurrying to the support of a noun, when the hem of his jacket was pulled, and he stopped. "Surely," he said, in an undertone, "the time ain't up?" The man next him replied, "Oh, ain't it though?" rather caustically.

"Friends," said Herbert resuming his quiet voice, "I'm afraid I've kept you rather long. We've had opportunities before of meetin' each other; we shall 'ave opportunities again. I 'ave only to add one word." The man next to him frowned up at him on hearing this ominous phrase. "It's my firm and steadfast opinion that we shall increase our power and magnify our strength only by sticking close, quite close, shoulder to shoulder, in what I may call the march of progress. Not otherwise shall we see the risin' sun salute the dawn—" (a momentary frown from the lame young woman had disconcerted him)—"of labour's triumph: not otherwise shall we—shall we—"

"Gain," prompted the young man next to him, sulkily.

"Gain—thank you—gain the respect of future ages and the admiration of posterity; not otherwise shall we lead others on in that battle which, to use the language of metaphor—"

"I say, old man," whispered his neighbour, "really! Play the game."

"I will not pursue the train of thought," said Erb, "on which I had, in a manner of speakin', embarked. One an' all, friends—thank you—kind 'tention—I now give way!"

"Feriends!" shouted the next man, stepping quickly on the chair, "our comrade from Berminsey has been so far carried away by his own eloquence as to overstep his time. In these circs, I will abstain from all preliminary remarks and come to the point at once. First of all, 'owever—"

The bowler hatted men, who had spoken, seemed bored now with the proceedings, and tried to make out the exact time by the clock on the great biscuit factory; unable to do this, they appealed to Erb, who, heated with his oratorical efforts, and gratified to notice that the tall young woman had limped away directly that he had finished, produced a smart silver watch and gave the required information. They spoke in an undertone of the evening's engagements: one proud man was to turn on the gas, as he cheerfully expressed it, at Victoria Park in the afternoon, another had had a long talk with a member of Parliament, and the member had shaken hands with him, "Quite 'omely and affable"; they all presented to the crowd a very serious and thoughtful and statesmanlike appearance as they whispered to each other. Flakes of the crowd began to fall away. The last speaker finished, hoarse and panting.

"Whose turn is it to carry the chair?"

"Erb's!" said the others, quickly.

"But I thought—" he began.

"You thought wrong," said the others. "Besides you're going straight 'ome."

They walked across the grass to the gates near the station, where men and children, and men with babies perched on their shoulders, were making way back to the homes from which they had been temporarily expelled in order to give wives and mothers opportunity for concentrating minds on the preparation for dinner.

"No use trying to blister you for 'alf a pint, Erb?"

"Waste of time," said Erb.

"What d'you do with all your money?"

"I don't find no difficulty," he replied, "in getting rid of it. Any spare cash goes in books. I've got a reg'lar little library at 'ome. John Stuart Mill and Professor Wallace and Robert Owen, and goodness knows what all."

"The only reely sensible thing you've done, Erb," remarked one, "is not getting married."

"That's one of 'em," he admitted.

"You don't know what it is to be always buying boots for the kiddies."

"Don't want."

"You single men get it all your own way. Same time, it's a selfish life in my opinion. You don't live for the sake of anybody."

"I live for the sake of a good many people," said Erb, dodging into the road to evade a square of girls carrying hymn books, and returning with his chair to the pavement. "What I'm anxious to do is to see the world better and brighter, to organise either by word of mouth or otherwise—"

"Old man!" protested the others indignantly, "give us a rest. You ain't in the park now."

He gave up the wooden chair to one of the men, who took it inside the passage of a house in Upper Grange Road. The others stepped across to a public house; he nodded and went on.

"Won't change your mind and 'ave one, Erb?"

"My mind," he called back, "is the one thing I never 'ardly change."

He did not relax his seriousness of demeanour until he had passed the high walled enclosure of Bricklayers' Arms Goods Station and had turned into Page's Walk. There the fact was borne on the air that dinner time was near, for attractive scents of cooking issued out of every doorway; he moved his lips appreciatively and hurried on with a more cheerful air. Women slipped along with their aprons hiding plates of well baked joints and potatoes: children waited anxiously in doorways for the signal to approach the one gay, over satisfying meal of the week, at which there was always an unusual exhibition of geniality and good temper that would eventually conciliate the worried mother, who had devoted the morning to providing the meal. Men returned from a morning at their clubs, where the hours had been chased by a third rate music hall entertainment; these walked slowly and hummed or whistled some enticing air with which they desired better acquaintance. Erb scraped his boots carefully on the edge of the pavement, and went up the stone steps of some model dwellings. From No. 17 came a broad hint of rabbit pie: a veiled suggestion of pickled pork.

"Well, young six foot," he said cheerfully, "is the banquet prepared, and are all our honoured guests assembled?"

"Wouldn't be you," remarked his short sister, quickly, "if you didn't come 'ome long before you were wanted." She stood on tiptoe and glanced at herself in the glass over the mantelpiece, and rolled up her sleeves again; her head was covered with steel hair curlers, which had held it fiercely since the previous morning. "And me in me disables."

"You look all right," said Erb.

"I shall 'ave to be this afternoon."

"What's going to 'appen this afternoon?

"I told you!" remonstrated his sister. "My new young man's going to drop in for a cup of tea."

"Which?"

"I never have more than one at a time."

"You mean the one in the hat place in Southwark Street."

"Bah!" said his young sister contemptuously. "I gave him the sack weeks ago."

"You're always a choppin' and a changin'," said Erb tolerantly.

"If you weren't such a great gawk," remarked his sister, bending to peep into the oven, "you'd put the knives and forks, and not sit there like a—like a—I don't know what."

Erb pulled a drawer underneath the table and complied.

"The other way about, stupid," said the short girl wrathfully. "You don't take your knife in your left hand, do you? 'Pon me word, I often wonder that men was ever invented. I s'pose you've been talkin' yourself 'ungry, as usual?"

"I addressed a large meeting," said Erb, with a touch of his important manner, "for upwards of eleven minutes."

"Did they aim straight?"

"They were very appreciative," said Erb. "One chap that interrupted I went for with 'orse, foot, and artillery."

"Did you, though?" asked his short sister with reluctant admiration. "Make him squirm, eh, Erb? Did ye call him names, or did you say something about his nose?"

"I treated him with satire!"

"Weren't there ladies present, then?"

"There was one, as it happened."

"She'd been better off at 'ome," remarked the girl severely. "The minx."

"She looked all right."

"You can't go by looks nowadays."

"A tremendous weapon satire in the 'ands of a clever man," said Erb exultantly, "takes the starch out of 'em like drenching with a fire 'ose. Am I supposed to stay on 'ere whilst this new chap of yours mops up his tea?"

"Unless me lady comes down from Eaton Square to lord it over us all."

"Nice occupation for a man of my—a man of my—"

"Don't say 'intellect,'" begged his sister. "Spoils me appetite if I laugh much before dinner."

A pleasure to watch the sister, her sleeves rolled up to the elbow, setting right the things on the table, placing, with the aid of an exact pair of eyes, the china cruet stand at the very centre, fabricating some mustard in a teacup, and pouring it cleanly and carefully into the mustard pot, glancing at the oven with an encouraging, "'Urry up there!" to the pie, and ever a wary look out on the lid of the saucepan on the fire; the intervals she filled by complaining of the price of coals, by dusting the mantelpiece, by asking questions about the morning's speeches, and by explaining with great interest the trouble that came to a girl in her workshop consequent on accepting engagement rings from two young men at the same time. Presently the one right moment arrived, and out came the rabbit pie, with a crust not to be equalled for lightness and flakiness in Page's Walk, where, indeed, experiments in the higher walks of cookery usually proved so disastrous as to lead to domestic contention and a review of all the varied grievances that had accumulated throughout the ages. Erb, at the head of the table, cut the pie, and his young sister sat at the side, with one foot on the insecure support, so that the table scarcely wobbled under this trying operation; there ensued some argument because Erb wanted to place both of the kidneys on her plate, and his sister would not hear of this, but a compromise was effected by sharing these dainties fairly and equally. His sister said grace.

"For what we are 'bout 'ceive, Lord make us truly thankful for."

"Well?" she asked, rather nervously, as Erb took his first mouthful. Erb tasted with the air of a connoisseur.

"I've tasted worse," he said.

"I was afraid how it was going to turn out," confessed his sister with relief. "It's long since I tried my 'and at a pie."

"There's nothing anyone can't do in this so called life of ours," said Erb oracularly, "providin' that we put our best into it. We've all been endowed—"

"Pickle pork all right?"

"The pickle pork isn't nearly so bad as it might be," said Erb. "They couldn't beat it in Eaton Square. As I was saying, the human brain—"

"If Alice comes down from Eaton Square this afternoon in anything new," said his young sister definitely, "I shall simply ignore it. In fact, I shall say, 'Oh, you haven't got anything new for the spring then yet?' That," said the girl gleefully, "that'll make her aspirate her aitches."

"We mustn't forget that she's our sister."

"She'd like to get it out of her memory. Being parlourmaid in Eaton Square, and about five foot ten from top to toe, don't entitle anybody to come down 'ere to Page's Walk and act about as though Bricklayers' Arms Station belonged to them. After all, she's only a servant, Erb; there's no getting away from that. She doesn't get her evenings to herself like I do. Compared with her, I'm almost independent, mind you. I may 'ave to work 'ard in the day, I don't deny it, but after seven o'clock at night I'm me own mistress, and I can go out and about jest as I jolly well like. Tip up the dish, and take some more gravy."

"As a matter of fact you come 'ome 'ere, and you work about and get the place ready against me coming 'ome."

"And why shouldn't I?" demanded his young sister warmly, "if I like to? Can't I please meself? I'd a jolly sight rather do that than go and wait at table on a lot of over dressed or under dressed people, and obliged to keep a straight face whatever silly things you might 'ear them say. Is there a little bit more of the crust you can spare me?"

"I quite admit," said Erb, supplying her offered plate, "that to me there is something distasteful—"

"I only put the leastest bit of onion in."

"I'm referrin' now to the arrangement by which those who possess riches are able to call upon the working portion of the population to enable them to live idle, slothful lives. I may be wrong, but it seems to me—"

"I don't blame them," remarked his sister quickly, with her involuntary twitching of the head. "I should do the same if I was in their place. Tapioca pudding, Erb, for after. How does that strike you?"

"A tapioca and me," said Erb genially, "have always been on speaking terms. I can always do with a tapioca. A tapioca and me are good chums. Don't forget your stout."

"Wish I was."

"What I mean is, don't forget to drink it. My friend Payne, by the way, may call with a message."

"I'd as lief take doctor's stuff," said his sister with a wry face. "What's Payne calling about?"

"Orgenisation," answered Erb mysteriously.

"Oh," she said casually, "that rot."

"You'll have a lay down after dinner."

"I shall be busy," answered his sister, "making meself good looking."

"You'll have a lay down," Erb repeated firmly. "Besides, you look all right. Your face is a bit white, but," with a burst of compliment, "you'd pass in a crowd. No cheese for me. You 'ave some."

"I've done, thanks." She bowed her head and spoke rapidly in an undertone "F," "What we have received the Lord make us—"

The fact that the tall sister from Eaton Square called before Louisa had changed and taken her hair out of curlers was attributed by Louisa to the tall sister's unvarying desire to see Page's Walk at its worst, to find thus excuse for showering upon it her contempt. Alice, from a lofty height added to by an astonishing hat from which Louisa could not, in spite of herself, keep her eyes, complained bitterly to her sister of the state of Old Kent Road, upbraided Erb for the impudence of a 'bus conductor who, because she had talked a little on the way, offered to carry her on to the Deaf and Dumb Asylum without extra charge. "The vulgar humour of these poor men," said Alice, unnecessarily dusting a chair before sitting down, "appals one." She mentioned that the Eaton Square coachman had offered to drive her anywhere she wanted to go, but that, for various reasons, into which she preferred not to enter, she had declined.

"I've brought you a bottle of Burgundy, Louisa. You'll find it in my muff."

"To put on me 'andkerchief?" asked Louisa satirically.

The tall sister glanced appealingly first at the stolid Erb, then at the ceiling.

"I am on good terms with the housekeeper," she explained, "for the moment, and there is no difficulty in obtaining any little thing of this kind. And you're not looking well. You want picking up."

"Your idea seems to be to give me a set down," said Louisa. "Going to take your things off?"

"I'll just loosen my jacket. I won't take it off, thank you."

"You know the state of the lining better than I do. Erb, you're silent all at once."

"I was thinking," said Erb, going across the room and taking the bottle from its resting place. "How much does a bottle of Burgundy wine like this run into, Alice?"

An exclamation came from the short girl as the tall sister took a pair of pince nez from her breast, and, with great care, put on these new decorations in order to assist her in giving the answer.

"A bottle like that would 'run into,'" she explained with a short laugh as she quoted Erb, "about, what shall I say, six or seven shillings."

"You can take it back," he said shortly.

"Bra vo, Erb," whispered Louisa.

"I'm not going to be indebted," said Erb, leaning his fists on the deal table, "to Eaton Square or any other haunt of the aristocracy for philanthropy of any kind or description whatever, not even when they are not aware that they're giving anything away. I should be stultifying meself if I did. If Louisa or me wants Burgundy we can buy it at the grocer's, and, if necessary, go as far as to drink it, with the satisfied feeling that we're not beholden to any one. Eh, Louisa?"

"You've hit it in once," agreed the short sister. "Cigar or coker nut?"

"Therefore, whilst thankin' you, one and all, for your doubtless well meant kindness, perhaps, Alice, you'll understand that my principles—"

"You needn't bang the table about," interrupted the tall sister.

"It's ours," retorted Louisa. "We can bang it if we like."

"My principles," repeated Erb with relish, "prevent me from accepting anything whatsoever concerning which I have reason to believe that it had not been acquired, or bought, or paid for by the party at whose hands—at whose hands–"

"That's right, Erb," said Louisa encouragingly.

"At whose hands that gift is, so to speak, attempted to be bestowed."

"I shall look pretty," protested Alice, "carrying that about all the evening."

"If it has that effect," said her short sister, "I don't see how you can grumble. Come in the bedroom and show me how you manage this new way of doing up the hair."

Erb read a chapter from Herbert Spencer whilst the girls were out of the room, well repaid if here and there he understood a sentence, or now and again caught sight of a view that soon eluded him. The book had been recommended by a speaker at the Liberal and Radical Club a few Sundays before, an Honourable Somebody, whose proud boast it was that he had unsuccessfully contested more seats at general and at bye elections than any man belonging to his party, and who was, indeed, such an uncompromising bore, that he might well and appropriately have been subsidized by his very grateful opponents. The Honourable Somebody had also strongly recommended a book by Ruskin, and this, too, Erb had procured from the Free Library, but had given it up after a brief struggle, confessing that it was a bit too thick even for him. Erb made notes on the back of parcels' waybills when he came on something that seemed to him lucid: smiled to think of the start his companions would give when they heard him say in a speech, "I am inclined to go with our friend Spencer and say with him—" conveying in this way an impression that his acquaintance with literature was so complete that he had but to pick and choose from the treasures of his memory in order to give an illuminating quotation. He had made a bag of five when his sisters returned to the front room; Louisa without her fierce hair curlers, her head decked out in a new fashion, and more amiable in her attitude towards her sister, and, indeed, holding her arm affectionately. Alice, with her hat off, slightly less austere, took up Erb's book with a word of apology and remarked, "Oh, yes!" in the manner of one recognising an old companion.

"Read it?"

"Well," said the tall sister, "I have not exactly read it, but I have heard of it. Two of our young ladies talk about it sometimes at meals: Lady Frances declares she can't understand half of it."

"It's easy enough," said Erb, "once you get the hang of the thing."

"What are the young ladies like, Alice, at your new place?" asked the short sister at the looking glass.

"I've often been going to tell you, but you'd never listen," complained Alice.

"Tell us now!"

They all became much interested in this subject, and even Erb put some elucidating questions. Louisa looked admiringly at her tall sister as Alice went from this to the subject of visitors to Eaton Square: young Lady Frances, it seemed, occasionally gave mixed dinners, where no one knew anybody else, and even Lady Frances herself did not insist on previous acquaintance: the passport to these was notoriety. From this subject to the servants' coming party of the following Thursday week was an easy stage. Thursday had been selected to fit the convenience of certain visitors whose establishments on that day closed early.

"Another foot or so," said Louisa gazing up at her sister, "and I might 'ave been in your shoes."

"Height isn't the only thing required. We shall be rather short of gentlemen, by the bye."

"I can quite understand that."

"I suppose, Erb," said Alice to her brother doubtfully, "you wouldn't care to come if I got you an invite? If you did, you'd have to remember that I told them you were an inspector: you mustn't make me look like a story teller."

"Not much in my line," growled Erb. "Besides, I've got a big job coming on that I mustn't tell you anything further about jest now."

"I'd get you asked, Louisa," she said candidly to her short sister, "if you looked better than you do. I don't think your work does you any good."

"I'm not in it for me health," retorted the other, her head giving its involuntary shake.

"I've advised her to try something else," agreed Erb, walking up and down the room. "She's only a bit of a girl, and the circumstances under which our female workers are compelled to carry on their duties amount to a species of white slavery which would not be tolerated in Russia."

"Loud cheers!" commented Louisa. "It's about time my young man was 'ere. If he can't keep his appointments I shall have to talk to him straight."

As though in answer to this threat a loud single knock came at the door.

"Let him wait a bit," said Louisa. "Do him good."

Another knock came and the girl went to the door to upbraid the caller for unmannerly impatience. She withdrew her head quickly.

"It's Payne," she announced to her brother.

"Deuce it is!" said Erb with excitement.

In the passage stood a man with a stiff, short, red beard, his upper lip shaven; near to him, a newer arrival, a nervous youth, with a wired flower in his coat, who asked shyly whether Miss Barnes happened by any chance to be at home.

"Trot in," said Erb, jerking his head. The nervous youth took off his hat and obeyed. "Well, Payne, old man," said Erb to the other.

"I've won the three old 'uns over," whispered the man with the red beard.

"Good on you!"

"They'll sign to morrow."

"And if the answer ain't satisfactory?"

"Then," said Payne in an undertone, with his hand guarding the words at his mouth, "then they'll follow our lead."

"And strike?"

"And strike!" said Payne.

CHAPTER II

London starts its day as freshly as the country, and in the early hours of a spring morning, before the scent of the tanning yards is awake, even Bermondsey seems pure and bright. The loads of vegetables strolling up Old Kent Road, the belated pockets of last year's hops coming, roped sky high, out of the gates of the goods station; the rapid barrows returning from Covent Garden with supplies of flowers and fruit for suburban shops—all these help. At half past seven comes a transition period. The day's work has begun and it has not begun. Every five minutes increases the haste of those who come out of the giant model dwellings, and up from the tributary roads; girls, as they run, stab at their hats; men, at a trot, endeavour in vain to light their pipes, but continue trying as they go, because matches are cheap and time is priceless. The law of compensation asserts itself: those who were merry last night and stayed out until half past twelve to sing their way joyously home are, in the morning, thoughtful or surly, whilst those who eluded the attractions of the club or public house rally them with much enjoyment on their obvious depression.

Erb, after the exaltation of Sunday night's meeting in St. George's Road, where his unreasonable hope to see again the tall, lame girl had been disappointed, but where he had received from one of the leading men in the labour world, grown white haired in the service, a gracious compliment ("I was like my enthusiastic friend Barnes, here, when I was a lad," the white haired man had said), Erb experienced a slight reaction to find that here was the old matter of fact world and—Monday morning! An independent set, because of the fact that for so many hours of the day they were their own masters, with a horse and van to take them about, and a vanboy for slave or despot, on Monday mornings carmen were specially curt of speech and unreliable of temper. In the stables was contentious dispute about horses, about the condition of the empty vans, about tardily arriving boys, about anything, in fact, that lent itself to disapproval. Erb's boy, William Henry, was prompt as ever, but Erb found annoyance in the circumstance that his friend Payne, instead of taking up conversation in regard to an important matter where it had been left the previous afternoon, now treated this as a subject of secondary importance, and as they drove up in the direction of town and the Borough, insisted, with the interruptions that came when traffic parted their vans, on giving to Erb details of a domestic quarrel, in which his wife, Payne said, had been wrong and he had been right; Payne seemed anxious, however, to obtain confirmation of this view from some impartial outsider. The boy on each van left his rope at the back to listen.

"Shall we have time to do that," asked Erb at St. George's Church, where there was a stop of traffic, "before we start out on our first rounds? I should like to see it under weigh."

"It isn't," said Payne from his van, still absorbed with his own affairs, "it isn't as though I was always nagging. I don't seepose I've lifted me 'and at her half a dozen times this year, and then only when she's aggravated me."

"It ought to have an effect if we can get every name signed to it."

"Question is, has a legally married wife got any right to go throwing a man's rel'tives in his face jest because they don't come to see her? I ain't responsible for my Uncle Richard, am I? If he's gone and got himself into trouble in his time it ain't me that's got to be punished, is it? Very well, then, what's the use of talkin'?"

William Henry, in Erb's van, made a note. Never have an Uncle Richard.

"It must be unanimous," remarked Erb, speaking in fragments, and endeavouring to entice Payne's mind to imperial subjects as the policeman's hand allowed them to go on, "or else it might as well not be done at all. It's a case of all of us sticking together like glue. If it don't have no effect, what I've been thinking of is a deputation to the General Manager."

"She's not a going to manage me," returned Payne, catching something of the last sentence. "If I'm treated with proper respect I'm a lamb, but if anyone attempts to lord it over me, I'm simply a—"

William Henry, ordered back to the tail of his van, made note number two. Trouble brewing, and, in the case of wholesale discharges, a fair chance of honest lads gaining promotion.

The van foreman waited at the entrance to the railway arch where the up parcels office, after many experiments in other places, had decided to settle; he looked on narrowly as the vans drove up the side street. The van foreman had been a carman in his day (to say nothing of a more lowly start in boyhood), and he openly flattered himself that he knew the whole bag of tricks: he also sometimes remarked acutely that anyone who had the best of him had only one other person to get over, and that other person did not live on this earth. The van foreman was not really so clever as he judged himself to be (but his case was neither unprecedented nor without imitators), and his maxim—which was that in dealing with men you had to keep hammering away at them—was one that in practice had at times defective results.

"Yes," said the van foreman gloomily, as though replying to a question, "of course, you two are not the first to arrive. Barnes and Payne—Payne and Barnes. There ain't a pin to choose between you. What's your excuse?"

"Wh oh!" said Erb to his horse, assuming that it had shied. "Wo—ho! my beauty. Don't be frightened at him. He ain't pretty, but he's quite harmless."

"I want no sauce," snapped the van foreman. "Good manners cost nothing."

"You might as well replenish your stock, then," retorted Erb.

"Re plenish!" echoed the other disgustedly. "Why don't you talk the Queen's English like what I do? What's all this I 'ear about a round robin to the guv'nor?"

"Fond of game, isn't he?"

"Look 'ere," said the van foreman seriously, "I'm not going to bemean meself by talking to you. I've spoken to some of the others, and I've told them there's the sack for every man jack of 'em that signs it. I give no such warning to you, mind: I simply turn me back on you, like this."

"Your back view's bad enough," called Erb as the other went off; "but your front view's something awful."

"I was a better lookin' chap than you," called the van foreman hotly, "once."

"Once ain't often," said Erb.

He backed his van into position, and was about to cry, "Chain on!" but William Henry had anticipated the order, and had, moreover, fetched from the booking up desk the long white delivery sheet, with its entries of names and addresses.

William Henry also assisted in loading up the parcels with more than usual alacrity, that he might have a few minutes in which to saunter about with an air of unconcern and pick up news concerning possible vacancies. The carmen who had finished their work of loading, went up to the further end of the arch, waiting for the hour of twenty to nine, and snatching the opportunity for discussing a matter of public interest. Erb followed, watched keenly by the van foreman.

"Got the document, Erb?"

"'Ere it is," said Erb importantly, drawing a long envelope from the inside pocket of his uniform jacket. "All drawn up in due order, I think."

"What we've got to be careful about," said a cautious, elderly carman preparing to listen, "is not to pitch it too strong, and not to pitch it too weak."

"The same first class idea occurred to me," remarked Erb.

"Read it out to 'em, Erb," suggested Payne.

Pride and a suggestion of Southwark Park was in the young man's tones, as, unfolding the sheet of foolscap paper, he proceeded to recite the terms of the memorial. The style was, perhaps, slightly too elaborate for the occasion, but this appeared to be no defect in the eyes and ears of the listening men.

"'And your petitioners respectfully submit, therefore, these facts to your notice, viz.,'—"

"What does 'viz.' mean?" asked the cautious, elderly carman.

"'Viz,'" explained Erb, "is quite a well known phrase, always used in official communications. 'To your notice, viz., the long hours which we work, the paucity of pay, and the mediocre prospects of advancement. Whilst your petitioners are unwilling to resort to extreme measures, they trust it will be understood that there exists a general and a unanimous determination to improve or ameliorate'—"

"He'll never understand words like that," said the elderly carman despairingly. "Why, I can only guess at their meaning."

"'Or ameliorate the present environments under which they are forced to carry on their duties. Asking the favour of an early answer, We are, sir, your obedient servants—'"

"That," concluded Erb, "that is where we all sign."

"Your respectful and obedient servants, I should say," suggested the elderly carman.

"Hark!" said Erb authoritatively. "The terms of this have all been very carefully considered, and once you begin to interfere with them, you'll mar the unity of the whole thing. Payne, got your pen?"

Payne seemed to feel that he was adjusting his quarrel with domestic events by dipping his penholder into an inkstand and signing his name fiercely. Erb followed, and the other men contributed to the irregular circle of names. The elderly carman hesitated, but one of his colleagues remarked that one might as well be hung for a sheep as a lamb, and the elderly carman appeared to derive great encouragement from this, signing his name carefully and legibly, and looking at it when done with something like affection.

"I sha'n't ask you to get away with your loads many more times," shouted the van foreman from the other end of the arch. "Yes, it's you I'm talkin' to. You're all champion mikers, every one of you. I wouldn't give three 'apence a dozen for you, not if I was allowed to pick and choose."

The men flushed.

"Chaps," said Erb quickly, "there's only one thing we might add. Shall we recommend that this old nuisance be done away with? I can easily work it in."

"I beg to second that," growled Payne.

"Thought you wasn't taking any suggestions?" remarked the elderly carman.

"This is more than a suggestion," said Erb masterfully. "Are we all agreed?" The men held up their hands, shoulder high. "Much obliged! Payne, after you with that pen."

Many of the van boys had snatched the opportunity to have a furtive game of banker with picture cards, but William Henry stood precisely at the tail of his mate's van, responding in no way to the raillery of his young comrades, who, in their efforts to move him from the path of good behaviour, exhausted a limited stock of adjectives, and a generous supply of nouns. To William Henry, as a safe lad, was entrusted the duty of taking the long envelope to the Chief's office, and his quick ears having gained something of the nature of the communication, he ran, and meeting the Chief at the door of the private office, gave it up with the message, "Answer wanted sharp, sir!" a gratuitous remark, ill calculated to secure for it an amiable reception.

The labour member who had given to Erb a golden compliment on the previous evening had many proud titles; he was accustomed to say that the one he prized highest was that of "a manager of men," and, indeed, the labour member had lost the colour of his hair and added lines to his face by piloting many a strike, guiding warily many a lock out, but he had been rewarded by the universal acknowledgment that he could induce the men to do as he wished them to do; having gained this position, any idea of revolt against his command appeared, on the face of it, preposterous. It pleased Erb, as he drove his soberly behaved horse and his van through the City to commence deliveries in the Pimlico district, to think that he, too, at the very outset, had impressed the colleagues with a confident manner. It was fine to see the wavering minds pin themselves to his superior direction, and give to him the duty of leading. He rehearsed to himself, as he drove along the Embankment, the speech which he would make when they held a meeting consequent on a refusal of the application; one sentence that came to his mind made him glow with delight, and he felt sure it had occurred to no one before. "United we must succeed; divided we most certainly shall fail!" He talked himself into such a state of ecstasy (William Henry, the while, swinging out by the rope, and repelling the impertinent action of boys driving shop cycles, who desired to economise labour by holding on at the rear of the van), that when he drove his thoughtful horse round by the Houses of Parliament it seemed to him that if the House were sitting he had almost achieved the right to get down and go in there and vote. At his first delivery to a contumacious butler, ill tempered from an impudent attempt on the part of his master to cut down expenses, recalled Erb to his actual position in life, and as he went on Grosvenor Road way he was again a carman at twenty three shillings and sixpence a week. Later, at a coffee shop which proclaimed itself "A Good Pull up for Carmen," and added proudly, "Others Compete, Few Equal, None Excel," he stopped for lunch, having by that time nearly finished his first round of deliveries.

He shouted an order of "Bag on!" to William Henry, and, stepping down, went inside. Other drivers from other companies were in the coffee house, and Erb, taking a seat in one of the pews, listened with tolerant interest to their confused arguments. All the variously uniformed men had a grievance, and all were quite certain that something ought to be done. The least vague of all the preferred solutions came from a North Western man, who said that "We must be up and doing."

"The great thing is," went on the North Western man, encouraged by the absence of contradiction, "to keep on pegging away."

"Which way?" asked the carman at the end of the room.

"That," said the North Western man modestly, "that it is not for me to decide. I leave that to wiser men than me. I candidly confess that I'm not one of your busybodies."

"Seems to me," remarked a Great Western man, cutting the thick bacon on his bread gloomily, "that every other department's getting a look in excepting the drivers. We're out of sight part of the day, and out of mind all the day. Take my own case. I've got children growing up, and I find," here the Great Western man rapped the handle end of his knife on the table, "I find they all want boots."

"What can I get for you?" said the matronly waitress, coming down the aisle.

"I didn't call you, my dear. I was only arguin'."

"Man like!" said the waitress, going back to the kitchen.

"I find 'em in boots," went on the man, "but do I ever 'ave a chance of seeing the kids 'cept Sunday?" A murmur of anticipatory agreement with the coming answer went round. "My youngest is about a year old, and takes notice in a manner that's simply wonderful—my wife says so, everybody says so, but he forgets me from one Sunday to another, and screams like anything when he catches sight of me."

"P'raps you smile at him, old man?"

"And that's why I agree," concluded the Great Western man earnestly, "that some'ing ought to be done. Has anybody got 'alf a pipe of 'bacca to spare?"

"What we want," remarked the North Western man, "is a chap that'll persuade us to—"

"Yes, but—after you with the metch, old sort—but where is he?"

Erb closed the black shiny bag which his sister Louisa had packed and stood out in the gangway between the pews. He held his peaked cap in his hand, and fingered at the brass buttons of his waistcoat.

"I've took the liberty of listening," he said, speaking slowly, "to the remarks you chaps have been making, and if there's two minutes to spare, I should like to offer my views. I sha'n't take more'n two minutes."

"Fire away," said the others, leaning out of their pews.

"Let me first of all preface my observations by telling you what we have done only this morning at my place. We have simply—" Erb described the procedure; the men listened interestedly. "And now let me tell you, friends, what we propose to do when this round robin of ours gets the usual sort of answer. We shall fix on a certain morning—this is in confidence, mind. We shall resolve upon a certain, definite, and final course of action. Then it'll be war, and we shall find out who's master."

"And s'posing they are?"

"They would stand no chance," cried Erb, "if we could but preserve a united front. But you're too nervous, all of you, to do that. You've been tied up, hand and foot, too long to know how to move. It will be for us at our place to show you a lead, and I can only 'ope for your sakes that when we prove successful you will 'ave the common sense, the energy, and the intelligence to go and do likewise. Meanwhile, so long!"

He punched at the inside of his peaked cap and strode out of the doorway, an exit that would have been dignified had not the stout waitress hurried down after him with a demand for fourpence halfpenny. Even in these circumstances, he had the gratification of hearing inquiries, "Who is he, who is he?" And one commendatory remark from the North Western man, "Got his 'ead screwed on the right way."

"Now, why ain't you lookin' after the van, William Henry?" asked Erb appealingly.

"I'm very sorry, mate," said the boy, "but I never can resist the temptation of listening to you."

Erb accepted the explanation. He climbed up to his seat, and, awakening the well fed horse, induced him to finish the deliveries. Eventually he drove back to the station. There he heard the latest news. The Chief had sent for the Van Foreman, a cabinet council had been held, the Chief had gone now to consult the General Manager. So far, good; the dovecotes had been fluttered. He met five or six of the carmen as he waited for his second deliveries, and criticised the writing of the clerk at the booking up desk; they were nervous now that the arrow had been shot, and they impressed upon Erb the fact that it was he who really pulled the bow. He accepted this implication of responsibility, his attitude slightly reassured the nervous. A young horse was brought up from the stables to take the place of the solemn animal, and its eccentric and sportive behaviour served to occupy Erb's thoughts during the afternoon. He had occasion to deliver a hamper of vegetables at a house in Eaton Square, and to collect a basket of laundry, and as he waited he saw his sister Alice on the steps of her house whistling for a hansom; he would have offered assistance, only that he remembered that in the eyes of that house he was an Inspector; when a cab answered the appeal a very tall, neatly dressed young woman came down the steps, preceded by Alice, who ran to guard the muddy wheel with a basket protector. An attractive face the tall young woman had. Erb would have thought more of it, but for the fact that at this period of his career he had determined to wave from his purview all members of the fair sex, excepting only his sisters; the work before him would not permit of the interference that women sometimes gave. He resented the fact that the lame young woman of Southwark Park would not go from his memory. Erb reproved him sharply, and ordered him to mind his own business.

"Carman Barnes. To see me here, on to day, certain."

This was the endorsement in red ink on the sheet of blue foolscap which had set out the grievances of the carmen, and Erb flushed with pride to find that he, and he alone, had been selected to argue the grievances of his colleagues with the Chief of the department. The men appeared not to grudge him the honour, and the van foreman held himself austerely in a corner, declining to open his mouth, as though fearful of disclosing an important state secret. Erb thought it diplomatic to ask the others whether they had any suggestions to offer for the coming debate (this without any intention of accepting advice); they all declared moodily that it was he who had led them into trouble, and his, therefore, should be the task of getting them out. Payne wished him good luck, but appeared to have no great confidence in his own powers of prophecy. Erb washed in a zinc pail, parted his obstinate hair carefully with the doubtful assistance given by a cheap pocket mirror which William Henry always carried, and, watched by the carmen and chaffed by the casually interested porters and clerks, he went to endure that experience of an interview with the Chief, known as "going on the carpet." The Chief was engaged for the moment; would Carman Barnes please wait for a few moments? It happened that Erb himself was boiling for the consultation, and this enforced delay of a few moments, which grew into ten minutes, disconcerted him; when at last a shorthand clerk came out, and he was admitted into the presence, some of his warm confidence had cooled. The Chief, a big, polite, good tempered man, sat at the table signing letters.

"Shan't keep you half a second," he remarked, looking up.

"Very good, sir."

"Beautiful weather," said the Chief absently, as he read, "for the time of the year."

"We can't complain, sir," said Erb meaningly, "of the weather." The clock up high on the wall of the office ticked on, and Erb endeavoured to marshal his arguments in his mind afresh.

"That little job is finished," said the Chief, dabbing the blotting paper on his last signature. "I wonder how many times I sign my name in the course of a day; if only I had as many sovereigns. Let me see, what was it we wanted to talk to each other about?" Erb produced the memorial, and stood cap in hand as the Chief read it with an air that suggested no previous knowledge of the communication. "Oh, yes," said the Chief, "of course. I remember now. Something about the hours of duty."

"And wages," said Erb, "et cetera."

"I get so much to think of," went on the Chief, autobiographically, "that unless I put it all down on a memo I forget about it. Now when I was your age. What are you, Barnes?"

"Twenty one next birthday, sir."

"Ah," sighed the Chief, "a fine thing to be one and twenty, you've got all the world before you. You ought to be as happy as a lord at your age."

"The 'appiness that a lord would extract from twenty three and six a week would go in a waistcoat pocket."

"There's something in that," admitted the other, cheerfully. "But, bless my soul, there are plenty worse off. A man can grub along very well on it so long as he is not ambitious."

"And why shouldn't a man be ambitious?" demanded Erb. "Some people raise themselves up from small beginnings"—the Chief took up his paper cutter—"and all honour to them for it." The Chief laid down the paper cutter. "It must be a great satisfaction to look back when they are getting their three or four 'undred a year and think of the time when they were getting only a quid a week. It must make 'em proud of themselves, and their wife and their women folk must be proud of 'em too."

"Married, Barnes?"

"No, sir. Live with my sister."

"Engaged perhaps?"

"Not on twenty three and six."

Difficult to use the well rehearsed arguments and the violent phrases to a courteous man, who showed so much personal interest. If he would but raise his voice or show defiant want of sympathy.

"But some of us are married, sir," Erb went on, "and some of us have children, and I tell you straight, when the rent is paid, and when the children's clothes are bought and just the necessaries of life are purchased, there's precious little left over. You can't realise perhaps, sir, what it means to look at every penny, and look at it hard, before it's paid away."

"Pick up a bit, don't you, you carmen?"

"An occasional twopence," cried Erb, "and think what a degrading thing it is for some of us to accept voluntary contributions from those placed in a more fortunate position in life?"

"Never knew a railway man object to it before," mused the Chief.

"You're thinking of the old school, sir. Men are beginning to recognise that capital can't do without them, and capital must therefore fork out accordingly. This memorial which you hold at the present time in your 'and, sir, contains a moderate appeal. If that moderate appeal is refused, I won't be answerable for the consequences."

"And yet, I take it, you know more about the consequences than anyone else?"

"Be that as it may, sir," said Erb, flattered, "we needn't go into hypo—hypo—"

"Hypothetical?"

"Thank you, sir. We needn't go into that part of the question at present. But it's only fair to warn you that when I go back to the men and tell them that their very reasonable applications have been one and all refused, and refused, if I may say so, with ignominy, then there'll be such an outbreak. Mind you, sir, I'm not blaming you; I only talk to you in this way, because 'ere's me representing labour on this side of the table, and there's you on the other side of the table representing capital."

"Labour," remarked the Chief, trying to make a tent of three pen holders, "is to be congratulated."

"Therefore, not wishing to take up your time any longer, I should like to conclude by remarking in the language of one of our poets of old, who remarks—"

"No, no," protested the Chief gently, "don't let us drag in the poets. They were all very well in their way, but really you know, not railway men. Not one of them. What I want you to tell the others is that if I had the power of deciding on this matter, likely enough I should give them everything they ask. But above me, Barnes, above me is the Superintendent, above the Superintendent is the General Manager, above the General Manager are the Directors, and above the Directors are the Shareholders."

"And all of you a stamping down on poor us."

"To a certain extent," admitted the Chief, in his friendly way, "but only to a certain extent. What they want, what I want, is that everything should go on smoothly."

"To come to the point," suggested Erb. "I take it that you answer this application, sir, in the negative. I take it that I'm to go back to the men and say to them, 'All my efforts on your behalf have been fruitless.'"

"Your efforts?"

"My efforts," said Erb proudly.

"You are mainly responsible then?"

"I don't deny it."

"I see," said the Chief, slowly pulling the feathers from a quill pen. "My information was to that effect, but it is well to have it confirmed by you. Now look here, Barnes." He took up the sheet of blue foolscap, with a change of manner. "The men ask for the removal of the van foreman. That suggestion will not be acted upon. If we were all to be allowed to choose our own masters we should be playing a nice topsy turvy game. You understand?"

"I've taken a note of it," remarked Erb darkly. He wrote something with a short pencil on the back of an envelope. "Negative answer also, I s'pose, to the question of hours?"

"Not so fast. In regard to the question of hours some concession will be made. They have increased of late without my knowledge. The men will take it in turns, in batches of three or four, to go off duty at six o'clock one week in the month. This will necessitate a couple of extra carmen."

"Good!" approved Erb, making a fresh note. "We now approach the question of wages."

"The men who have been in the service for five years will receive an additional two shillings a week."

"That's a fair offer."

"The men who have been with us for more than a year will, with one exception, receive an increase of one and six."

Erb wrote the figures on the back of the envelope. Already he was composing in his mind the elaborate sentences by which he would make the satisfactory announcement to his colleagues. A telephone bell in the corner of the office stung the ear; the Chief rose, and bidding Erb wait outside for a few minutes, went to answer it. Erb closed the door after him in order to avoid any suspicion of overhearing, and, big with the important news, could not resist the temptation to hurry through into the arch where the men in a group were waiting; the van foreman sat on a high stool in the corner, in an attitude that suggested contrition.

"Well, chaps," said Payne, when Erb, in one long, ornate sentence had given the information, "this is a little bit of all right. I think I'm speaking the general opinion when I say we're very much indebted to Erb for all the trouble he's took."

"Hear, hear!" said the men cheerfully.

"I could see from the first," remarked the eldest carman, "that he meant to pull it off for us."

"The occasion being special," said Payne, bunching his short, red beard in one hand, "I think we might all of us treat ourselves to a tonic."

"Not me," said Erb. "I've got to get back just to say a few words to the gov'nor. But don't let me stop you chaps from 'aving one."

"You won't!" remarked Payne with candour.

The conversation at the telephone was still going on when Erb returned to the Chief's office; some time having been occupied, apparently, with the usual preliminaries of one party begging the other to speak up, and the other urging on the first the advisability of seeking some remedy for increasing deafness. The Chief rang off presently, and came to the door and opened it.

"Sorry to keep you waiting, Barnes."

"Was there anything else you wanted to say, sir?"

"Only this. I told you there was one exception in this scheme of increases."

"Everitt is a bit too fond of the glass, sir, but p'raps a word of warning from you—"

"Everitt drinks, but Everitt does his work quietly, and he doesn't disturb the other men. The one exception, Barnes, is yourself."

"Me?" exclaimed Erb.

"It's like this," said the Chief, going on with the work of plucking a quill pen. "You're a restless organiser, and no doubt somewhere in the world there is a place for you. But not here, Barnes, not here! Of course, we don't want to sack you, but if you don't mind looking out for another berth—No hurry, you know, next week will do—why—"

The Chief threw down the stark quill pen; intimation that the conference was at an end.

"I'm not the first martyr that's suffered in the cause of right and justice," said Erb, his face white, "and I'm probably not the last. I take this as a distinct encouragement, sir, to go on in the path that Fate has mapped out for me, ever striving, I trust, not so much to improve my own personal position, as to better—"

"Shut the door after you," said the Chief, "and close it quietly, there's a good chap."

CHAPTER III

Turmoil of the mind that followed in the next few days was increased by the worry of a Society engagement. To the servants' party in Eaton Square, Erb, having been formally invited, sent answer that he was busy with meetings of one sort and another, and begged, therefore, to be excused: this to his sister Louisa's great content. Arrived another post card from Alice, saying that if this meant that he would not come unless Louisa were invited, then she supposed there was nothing to do but to ask them both; she would send a few things down by Carter Paterson the day before the party, that Louisa might adorn herself with something like distinction, and do as little harm as possible to the repute of Alice. To this, after an enthusiastic discussion, that was not a discussion, in that Louisa did all the talking, a reply was sent, stating that Louisa and himself would arrive by a series of 'buses on the night mentioned, and that Louisa begged her sister would not deprive herself of articles of attire, "me having," said Louisa's note, "ample." The incident had its fortunate side, insomuch that it absorbed the whole mind of the delighted young sister, and prevented her from giving much attention to the matter of Erb's forced resignation. Lady experts called every evening at the model dwellings to give advice in regard to costume, and, in the workshop, other white faced girls pushed aside the relation of their love affairs in order to give their minds to this subject: Louisa's current young man received stern orders not so much as dare show his face in Page's Walk for a good fortnight. It was only on the evening of the party, when Louisa, gorgeously apparelled, sat in the living room, ready a full hour before the time for starting, and Erb in his bedroom about to start on the work of changing from a parcels carman to a private gentleman, that the short girl found leisure and opportunity to review Erb's affairs.

"And all the rest," said Louisa severely in conclusion, "all the rest of these 'umbugs reaping the fruits of your labours, and you thrown out neck and crop. I can't think how you come to be such a idiot. You don't see me doing such silly things. What do you think your poor mother would say if she were 'ere?"

"You haven't seen the evening paper, I s'pose?" asked the voice of Erb, muffled by soap suds.

"Evening paper," echoed the short sister, fractiously. "Is this a time for bothering about evening papers? The question is what are you going to do next, Erb? Been round to any of the other stations?" A grunt from the bedroom intimated a negative answer. "You'll come to rack and ruin, Erb, that's what you'll come to if I don't look after you."

"Catch hold." A bare arm held out from the bedroom doorway a pink evening paper.

"What d'you want me to read now? I don't want to go botherin' my 'ead about murders when I'm full of this party."

"Where my thumb is," said Erb's voice. A damp mark guided her attention, and she read it, her lips moving silently as she went through the paragraph, her head giving its uncontrollable shake.

"We understand that a Society of Railway Carmen has been formed, and that the first meeting will be held at the Druid's Arms, Southwark, on Saturday evening, at half past nine o'clock, a late hour fixed in order to secure the attendance of the men. There are two candidates for the position of secretary—Messrs. Herbert Barnes and James Spanswick. The former is losing his situation for taking part in a labour movement, and his case has excited a great deal of interest."

"I say," cried Louisa, in an awed voice, "that's never meant for you, Erb?"

"It ain't meant for anyone else," called Erb. "Seen anything of my stud?"

"Where did you put it last? But, just fancy, in print too. And underneath is something about Royalty." Louisa clicked her tongue amazedly. "You never said anything about it, either."

"No use talking too much. Why, here's the collar stud in the shirt all the time. No use talking too much beforehand. Besides, it isn't what you may call definitely settled yet. Spanswick's got very strong support, and he hates me as much as he likes beer. I said something rather caustic on one occasion about his grammar."

"I shall snip this out," said Louisa, as Erb appeared struggling into his coat, "and I shall show it privately to everybody I come across in Eaton Square to night."

"I don't know that that's worth while," he said doubtfully.

"It'll let 'em see," said Louisa, with decision, "that they ain't everybody. When you've done trimming your cuffs with the scissors—"

No further word of disparagement came from the short girl as she trotted along proudly by the side of her brother to the junction where New Kent Road starts for Walworth and town. Indeed, outside the tram she expressed some surprise at the fact that so many people were not acquainted with her brother; she consoled herself by the assurance that once Erb obtained a start the whole world would join her in an attitude of respect; she also enjoyed, in anticipation, the reflected glory that would be hers in the workshop the following morning. Being as outspoken in praise as in blame, it resulted, as they walked over Westminster Bridge and took an omnibus, that not only Louisa, but Erb himself, had attained a glowing state of content, and when they arrived eventually at the house in Eaton Square (lighted recklessly below and sparsely illuminated above) they felt that the world might possibly contain their equals, but they were certainly not prepared to look on anybody as a superior.

"Jackson," said the buttoned boy who opened the door as they descended the area, "this looks like your lot."

"They call her Jackson," whispered Louisa to her brother, interrupting his protest. "Parlour maid here is always called Jackson."

Alice came forward. A spray of wild flowers meandered from the waist of her pale blue dress to her neck; she took her brother's hand up high in the air before shaking it. A few tightly collared young men stood about the entrance to the cleared kitchen, encouraging white gloves to cover their hands; they also had bunches of flowers in buttonholes, and one of them wore an open dress waistcoat. A Japanese screen masked the big range; nails in the walls had been relieved of their duties, a white cloth'd table with refreshments stood at the end near a pianoforte.

"You're early," said Alice, kissing her sister casually. Louisa took the brown paper parcel from Erb's arm.

"Thought you'd like the evening to start well," she said. "Any gentlemen coming?"

"Haven't you got eyes?" asked Alice, leading the way upstairs and waving a hand in the direction of the shy youths.

"Gentlemen, I said," remarked Louisa.

"I shall begin to wish I hadn't asked you," said Alice pettishly, "if you're going on like that all the evening. I believe you only do it to annoy me."

"What else could I do it for?" asked the short sister.

"Erb," ordered the tall sister from the stairs, "you leave your hat and coat in that room. Thank goodness I've got a brother who knows how to behave. Good mind now not to titivate your hair for you."

"You mustn't mind me," said Louisa, relenting at this threat. "It's only me manner."

They were received on returning downstairs by the housekeeper, a large important lady in black silk and with so many chains that she might have been a contented inmate of some amazingly gorgeous and generous prison; the housekeeper having been informed that Erb was an official on a South of England railway begged him to explain why, in travelling through Ireland during the winter, it was so difficult to obtain foot warmers, and seemed not altogether satisfied with the reply that it was probably because the Irish railways did not keep them in sufficient quantities. The cook, also stout but short, engaged Erb for the first two dances, assuring him (this proved indeed to be a fact) that she was, in spite of appearances, very light on her toes, and quoting a compliment that had been paid to her by a perfect stranger, and therefore unbiased, at Holborn Town Hall in the early eighties.

"And this, Erb, is Jessie," said Alice, introducing a large eyed young woman in pale green. "Jessie is my very great friend." She added, "Just at present."

"I think you speak, Mr. Barnes?" said the large eyed young woman earnestly.

"I open my mouth now and again," admitted Erb, "just for the sake of exercising my face."

"Ah!" she sighed, looking at him in a rapt, absorbed way. "Somehow you put it all in a nutshell. I should simply love to be able to say the true, the right, the inevitable thing. I could almost—perhaps, I ought not to say it—but I could almost worship a clever man."

Erb, reddening, said that there were precious few of them about.

"Talk to me, please!" she said appealingly. "Button this glove of mine, and then tell me all about yourself. I shall be frightfully interested."

"You don't want to hear about me," said Erb, essaying the task set him.

"If you only knew!" she said.

This was really very gratifying. Erb had wondered whether the evening would interfere for a time with consideration of his great crisis: he soon found that the evening was to put that subject entirely out of his thoughts. This was in itself a relief, for, despite confidence in himself, he felt nervous about the result of the forthcoming meeting; to night he could dismiss worry and give his mind a holiday. He found that Jessie's surname was Luker, and the house called her Masters; the tall young woman declared that she positively hated the name of Luker, and confessed to a special admiration for the name of Barnes, strongly contesting Erb's suggestion that Barnes was a second class sort of name, and worthy of but little esteem. Near the cottage pianoforte that had been fixed in the corner of the kitchen, a sombre young person in black sat on a chair that had to be improved and made suitable by an enormous dictionary, fetched by the pageboy from upstairs, and, receiving orders to play just what she liked for the first, this lady struck violently into the prelude of a waltz, choosing a square in the pattern of the wall paper before her at which she could yawn. Couples, standing up, waited impatiently for the real waltz to commence; young women moving a smartly slippered foot; Louisa formulating her first protest against convention by saying aloud to her partner, a precise footman, "Oh, let me and you make a start!" The others said, "S s s h!" and watched the butler. The butler gave a pull at his yellow waistcoat and advanced solemnly to the housekeeper.

"Mrs. Margetson," he said, "I'm not so handy on me feet as I used to be, but I trust I may have the honour of opening the dance with you?"

"Mr. Rackham," replied the housekeeper with a slight bow, "thank you very much for asking, but, as you know, the leastest excitement makes my head a torture. Would you mind," with a wave of the fan, "asking Mamselle to take my place?"

"I shall have much plaisure," said the French lady's maid, promptly. "A deux temps or a trois temps, Meestair R rackham?"

"Leave it to you, Mamselle," replied the butler.

The two went half way round the kitchen before the other couples ventured to move: a nod from the housekeeper then gave permission. Erb found himself rather unfortunate at first, and this was his own fault, for, with his usual manner of taking charge, he endeavoured to pilot the agreeable Miss Luker and ran her into rocks and whirlpools and on to the quicksands of ladies' trains; it was only after the fourth disaster, when the fiancé of the upper housemaid (who was one of the tightly collared men and wore his short hair brushed forward in the manner of grooms) said to him audibly, "Not accustomed to drive, apparently!" that he permitted Miss Luker to take up the duty of guidance, and thereafter they went in and out the swinging dancers with no accident. Miss Luker was quite a marvellous young woman, for she could dance and talk calmly at the same time, a trick so impossible to Erb that, when he attempted it, he found he could only stammer acquiescence to some contestable theory advanced by his partner, or ejaculate some words in acceptance of an undeserved compliment.

"It seems like fate," sighed Miss Luker, as she saved Erb from sweeping the pianiste from her dictionary and chair, "but do you know you have exactly my step? It seems like fate," repeated Miss Luker, as the music stopped and couples began to walk around the room, "and it is fate."

"I don't quite follow you," said Erb, trying to regain his breath and dodging the long train of Mamselle. "To my mind, most things depend on us, and if we want anything to happen we can generally make it happen. Otherwise, where would ambition, and energy, and what not come in?"

"You mustn't talk above my head," said Miss Luker, winningly. "You forget how stupid we poor women are." An accidental lull came in the clatter of conversation.

"You're an exception," declared Erb.

His sister looked over their shoulders at him with surprise, and the footman giggled. The others, with an elaborate show of tact, began to speak hurriedly on the first subject that occurred to them, and the lady at the pianoforte, checked half way through a yawn, was ordered by the housekeeper to play a set of Lancers. Erb, in his life, had many trying moments, but none seemed so acute as this, when he had been caught paying a compliment to a lady. It was the first time he had ever done it, and when his self control returned, and, taking sides, he and cook went through the devious ways of the set dance, he warned himself to use more care in future. Nevertheless, some excuse could be urged: whenever he glanced at Miss Luker, now with the gloomy young man for partner, he found that her large eyes were looking at him, and she turned away quickly with great show of confusion. When the Lancers had, by gracious permission of the housekeeper, repeated its last figure, cook, beckoned aside by the footman, introduced her partner with due formality. Mr. Danks—the footman bowed.

"We—er—know each other by reputation, Mr. Barnes."

"Very kind of you to say so," said Erb.

"When you feel inclined for a cigarette," said the footman, "give me the tip. What I mean to say is—tip me the wink! They won't let us smoke here, but we can go into the pantry, or we can take a whiff round the square if you prefer it." Here the footman giggled, "I often wonder whether 'round the square' is a correct expression. Find any trouble, may I ask, in choosin' your language?"

"It comes to me pretty free," said Erb, "if I'm at all 'eated."

"Heated," corrected Mr. Danks, "heated! Before I went to my uncle's in Southampton Street, Camberwell, to take lessons, I used to drop 'em like—like anything."

"Never trouble about trifles meself."

"For public men like me and you," said Mr. Danks. He stopped a giggle, perceiving that what he had thought to be a humorous remark did not, judging from Erb's expression, really bear that character. "Like me and you," he went on, "the letter aitch is one of the toughest difficulties that we have to encounter. In my profession, at one time, it was looked on, to use your words, as a trifle. Those times, Mr. Barnes, are gone and done with. The ability to aspirate the letter aitch in the right place—in the right place, mind you—has done more to break down the barriers that separated class from class than any other mortal thing in this blessed world."

"I wonder, now," said Erb, with some interest, "whether you're talking rot, or whether there's something in what you say?"

"If you think anything more of it," said Mr. Danks, feeling in his waistcoat pocket, "take my uncle's card, and go on and chat it over with him."

"'Professor of Elocution. Declamation Taught!'" read Erb.

"His daughter knows you; heard you speak in Southwark Park."

"Not a lame girl?"

"If I hadn't gone to him," said Mr. Danks nodding affirmatively, "I should never have known how to recite."

"Nice drawback that would have been. So her name's Danks?"

"Rosalind Danks."

"Rosalind," repeated Erb thoughtfully.

"As it is," said the other with a giggle of satisfaction, "my 'King Robert of Sicily' gets me more invites out than I know what to do with. I suppose your sister has told you all about it."

"Talks of nothing else," declared Erb inventively.

To his surprise, Mr. Danks shook him very warmly by the hand, giggling the while with satisfaction, and, with the remark that he must now do the amiable to the remaining member of the family, left Erb and went across to Louisa—Louisa, flushed and almost attractive looking from the excitement of dancing. Erb calculated the distance between himself and the fair Miss Luker, and, with an attempt to imitate the easy manner of Mr. Danks, lounged across in her direction, but before he reached her three of the young men had formed up defensively, and Erb had to lean clumsily against the wall near to his short sister and her new companion. Mr. Danks had placed a footstool for Louisa.

"You are rather short," explained the excellently mannered footman.

"I stopped growin' a purpose," said Louisa, kicking the footstool aside.

"You don't resemble your sister at all."

"Mustn't let her hear you say that," remarked Louisa, "else she'll be mad."

"It's been a very dull season in town," said Mr. Danks regretfully.

"Have you been away, then?"

"I suppose you get a good many engagements, Miss Barnes? What I mean to say is, don't you find it a great tax? The demands of society seem to increase year by year."

"It's some'ing awful," agreed Louisa. "I shall be out again—let me see—"

"To morrow night?"

"In about six weeks' time, to a cantata at Maze Pond Chapel. Scarcely gives you time to breathe, does it?"

Alice perceived that her brother was growing moody in his solitude, and brought up to him the French lady's maid, who, discovering that he had once spent a day at Boulogne—conveyed to and fro by a free pass—talked to him vivaciously on the superiority of her native country over all others. The young woman at the pianoforte, aroused from a brief nap, was ordered to play a schottische.

At this point the evening suffered a check. It was Cook's fault. Cook, fearing that the hours were not moving with enough rapidity, suggested games; suggested also one called the Stool of Repentance. Necessary for one person to leave the room, and Mr. Danks being selected for this honour, went out, and the others thereupon selected libellous statements, of which Erb took charge.

"Come in, King Robert of Sicily," called Erb. Mr. Danks entered, and was ordered by Cook (hugging herself with enjoyment) to take a chair in the centre of the kitchen. "Someone says you're conceited."

"That's you," said Mr. Danks pointing to Alice.

"Wrong!" remarked Erb. "Someone says all the gels laugh at you."

"That's you," decided Mr. Danks, pointing at Cook. Cook now convulsed with amusement.

"Wrong again! Someone says you can't recite for nuts."

"I say," urged Mr. Danks, wriggling on the chair, "I'm as fond of a joke as anyone, but really—That sounds like you, miss." Louisa shook her head negatively.

"You're not lucky, old man. Someone says you'll never get married in all your life for the simple reason that no one wants you."

"That's you this time, at any rate," cried Mr. Danks, with melancholy triumph. And, as Louisa it was, the short young woman had to go out.

"Come in!" cried Erb, when the accusations had been decided upon. "Some of 'em have been making it warm for you, Louiser."

"I'll make it hot for them, Erb."

"Someone says you'd be a fine looking gel if you were twice as broad and three times as long."

"Cook!" exclaimed Louisa.

Cook, slightly disappointed at this swift identification, made her way out with a large sigh of regret at enforced exercise. It was determined now to show more ingenuity, and Cook had to knock two or three times ere permission could be given for her return.

"Someone says," remarked Erb, "that you're the finest woman in Eaton Square, bar none."

Cook laughed coquettishly. "That sounds like you, Mr. Barnes."

"No fear," said Erb. "Someone says that you'll get engaged some day—"

"What nonsense!" interrupted Cook delightedly.

"If you only wear a thick veil over your face."

"Look here!" said Cook definitely. "That's enough of it. If I find out who said that I shall make no bones about it, but I shall go straight upstairs and complain to Lady Frances, so there now."

"Someone says," Erb went on, "that you've got such an uncommon size mouth that it would take three men and a boy to kiss you."

"I don't want to lose me temper," said Cook heatedly, and speaking with no stops, "and I'm not going to but once I know who dared say that and I'll go to the County Court first thing to morrow morning and take out a summons against them people shan't go saying just what they like about me behind me back without having to prove every single—No, no, I'm not getting cross nothing of the kind but once I know who so much as dared—It's a silly stupid game and I can't think why it was ever suggested."

They were going back to dancing after this unsuccessful essay, when a quiet tap came at the door of the kitchen; and the couples, standing up to begin, suddenly released each other, the French lady's maid crying humorously, "Ciel! c'est mon mari!" Conversation ceased, and Cook bustled forward and opened the door.

"May I come in, Cook, I wonder?"

"Why," cried Cook; hysterical with delight, "as though you need ask, my dear, I mean, m'lady!"

It seemed to Erb that the West End possessed some exceptional forcing properties that made all of its young women grow tall. He stood upright, as though on parade, unconsciously following the lead given by the tightly collared men and by Mr. Danks. As the very tall young woman went across the silent room to the housekeeper his gaze followed her; he would have given half his savings to have been permitted to assume a light, unconcerned, and, if possible, a defiant manner.

"Do you know," she said brightly, "that I have not been down here since I was ten years old?"

"That's twelve years ago, Lady Frances," said the housekeeper. The housekeeper adjusted a bow at the white shoulders of the new arrival with an air of privilege.

"You sometimes used to let me bake things, didn't you, Cook?"

"I had to take care you didn't eat 'em," said Cook, admiring her from the opposite side of the room. The strain on severe countenances around the kitchen relaxed slightly. "The others," added Cook proudly, "don't remember. It was before their time, Lady Frances."

"And now that I am here," said Lady Frances, "it seems that I am to spoil your party." The servants and their visitors murmured, "Oh, no!" in an unconvincing way.

"What I thought was," she went on brightly, "that I might play to you."

"We have taken the liberty," said the housekeeper, "of hiring a musical person."

"But you will be glad of a rest," said Lady Frances, touching the pianiste on the hand and stopping her in a yawn. "When I was at school at Cheltenham I used to be rather good at dance music." She turned suddenly and looked down at Louisa. "Perhaps you play?"

"Me?" echoed Louisa confusedly. Louisa's sister Alice lifted her eyes in silent appeal to the fates. "I draw the line at a mouth organ." Her sister frowned at the ceiling. "And even that I'm out of practice with." Louisa found her handkerchief in a back pocket, and with some idea of hiding her confusion, rubbed her little nose vigorously.

"I think you have dropped this," said Lady Frances, stooping.

"Oh, that's only a bit out of this evening's newspaper. About my brother," added the girl.

"Really! May I read it, I wonder."

"Spell the words you can't pronounce," said Louisa. The room waited. Erb shifted his feet and endeavoured to look unconcerned.

"Are you—Are you Miss Spanswick, then?" pleasantly and encouragingly.

"Am I Miss Spanswick?" echoed Louisa with despair in her voice. "Give it 'old! This is my brother's name—Herbert Barnes—and, consequently, my name is Barnes. Not Spanswick."

"I see! tell me what can I play?"

"Play something you know," advised Louisa.

"Rackham! please suggest something."

"If it wasn't troubling your ladyship," said Mr. Rackham, taking off the dictionary, "and putting you to a great amount of ill convenience, I should venture to suggest—hem!—a set of quadrilles."

Something in the playing, once the couples had persuaded themselves to make up sets and to dance to such an august musician, that had escaped the art of the hired pianiste. An emphasis at the right place; a marvellous ability for bringing the music of each figure to an end just as the dancing ceased, so that there was no longer necessity for clapping of hands to intimate that further melody was useless, or to go on dancing with no music at all. For the next, Lady Frances played a well marked air for a new dance that had possessed town, and in this Miss Luker gave up her partner and undertook to teach Erb, who was not fully informed on the subject. It occurred to Erb, as he tried to lift his foot at the appointed moment, and prepared immediately afterwards to swing the agreeable upper housemaid round by the waist, that although his partner had modelled her style on that of the young woman seated at the pianoforte, there existed between them a long interval. Both had the same interested way of speaking, the same attention in listening, but, with Miss Luker, there seemed to be nothing at the back of the eyes. Erb, finding himself possessed with a hope that Lady Frances might presently speak to him, tried to compensate for this weakness by telling Miss Luker, when they were lifting one foot and swinging round at the far end of the kitchen, that the title meant nothing to him, and that, for his part, he preferred to mix with everybody on a common platform, to which Miss Luker replied, "Ah! that's because you're a railway man." Presently, in one of those sudden blanks of general talk that surprise the unwary, his raised voice was heard to say,—

"—Consequence is that the few revel in luxury, while the many—" He hesitated, and went on floundering through the silence. "Whilst the many 'ave not the wherewithal to buy their daily bread."

The awkward silence continued, broken only by the music from the pianoforte and the swishing of skirts.

"Erb," said his sister Alice, frowning over Mr. Danks's shoulder, "remember where you are."

"Exercise tack, my dear sir," recommended the butler. "Exercise tack."

"Even visitors," remarked the housekeeper severely, so that the young woman at the pianoforte should hear, "even visitors ought to draw the line somewhere. We can't help our opinions, but we can all stop ourselves from expressing them."

The music stopped, and the household looked rather nervously towards the chair, with an endeavour to ascertain whether the occupant had overheard the discordant remarks. To their relief, she leaned engagingly back, and beckoned to Louisa. Louisa, her head twitching with pride and agitation, went across the floor, and stood swinging her programme round and round.

"You can play!" admitted Louisa. "Where did you pick it up?"

"I want you to bring your brother over to me," said Lady Frances.

Quite useless for the kitchen to pretend that it was giving its entire mind to the subject of refreshments. The situation demanded their eyes and ears; they ate oblong pieces of cake in a detached way, rather as though they were feeding someone else; the housekeeper looked at Alice, and shook her head desolately.

"I have been reading about you," said Lady Frances in her alert, interested way.

"Licker to me how these things get into the papers," he mumbled.

"I should be tremendously interested in life," said the girl, "if I occupied your position. There's something sporting about it." She looked at him intently, and he rubbed his nose under a vague impression that it bore some defect. "I wish you the best of good luck."

"Then I shall have it," said Erb. Alice looked round the room triumphantly, as who should say, Now we are scoring. "Not acquainted much with the working classes, p'raps, me lady?"

"To my regret, no!"

"They're made up of all sorts," went on Erb, wishing that he dared to look at her white shoulders as she looked at his face, "and for the most part they are very easily led. It's only now and again that you find one step out of the common ruck." He hesitated, seeing no way out of the sentence except by a self congratulatory exit.

"If I should ever want to see through Bermondsey," she said, clasping her knee, her head up attractively, "will you be my guide?"

"It would be a proud moment," said Erb. He added, hastily, "For me, I mean."

"Cook, shall I play one more, and then go back upstairs and leave off bothering you?"

"The idea," said Cook reproachfully; "the idea, m'lady, of calling it botherin' us."

The others murmured polite sympathy with Cook's view, but when Lady Frances had played the four figures in a manner that seemed to Erb quite without flaw, she said good night, giving a special word to Louisa that made the short girl redden with delight; coming back to the doorway after Cook had seen her out to say to Erb:

"Won't forget your promise, will you?"

The dance finished at half past eleven, and the yawning pianiste went off to another engagement in Eccleston Street that began at midnight and was to last until the hour of four. The servants came up the steps of the area to see their visitors go, Alice now so proud of her brother that she declined to acknowledge the compliments of Mr. Danks, ignoring that gentleman's fervent assurance that she had been, as he expressed it, the belle of the evening.

"Good bye, Mr. Barnes," said Miss Luker fervently. She walked on a few steps with him. "This evening will always, always remain in my mind as a precious memory."

"I shan't forget it in a hurry."

"Oh, thank you for those words," whispered Miss Luker.

"Don't mention it."

"But promise. You won't think harshly of me, will you?"

"As a matter of fact, I don't suppose I shall 'ave time to think of you at all, 'arshly or otherwise. To morrow night there's an important meeting on, and—"

"But if you should want to write to me," went on Miss Luker, undeterred and looking back at the gossiping bunch of visitors near the area entrance, "let me know and I'll send you some addressed envelopes. We live in a censorious world, Mr. Barnes, and—Here comes your young sister. Think of me at four o'clock every afternoon, and I'll promise to think of you."

"Well, but," protested Erb, "what's the use?"

"Bah!" said Miss Luker, with a sudden burst of undisguised contempt, "I wouldn't be a dunderheaded man for anything."

CHAPTER IV

The third round of deliveries was finished, and, arrived at his last evening, Erb, coat and collar off, washed away the traces of work in the stable pail with the aid of some aggressive soft soap that seemed to have its own way in everything. He had brought with him that morning a parcel of private clothes, and just before going out with the six o'clock turn, he had changed, and had handed in the corduroy uniform. A relief to feel that he no longer wore the brass buttons of servitude; of late they had seemed to reproach him. He had driven round the Surrey side with the air of a sporting gentleman taking out his own horse and trap; the private clothes helped him to say his good byes with dignity to all, and especially to his old enemy, the van foreman.

"You would go on in your own tin pot way," said the van foreman regretfully, "no matter what I said. Your case ought to act as a warnin'."

"To you?"

"I should 'ave thought," said the van foreman, with a wistful air, "after all that's passed between us we might as well part good friends, at any rate."

"Look here, old chap," said Erb good temperedly, "I tried to out you, and you tried to out me; and you've got the best of it. I don't complain, but I'm not going to pretend I'm on friendly terms with a man when I ain't."

"That's what I say," retorted the van foreman argumentatively. "You've got no discretion."

The manners of William Henry had about them a fine blend of condescension; the lad came forward from the tail of the van and sat on a hamper, big with news. He had been approached that afternoon and informed that, consequent on the departure of Erb, there would be some changes, and would he, William Henry, accept the position of junior porter at fourteen shillings a week.

"I shall probably work on from that," said William Henry, "to some even higher position, and then on again. See? And if ever you want a friend, Erb—"

"I don't let boys call me Erb. Mr. Barnes, if you please."

"If I'm a boy," said William Henry thoughtfully, "I don't quite see where you're going to find your men. As I was a sayin', if ever you should be down in the gutter—and, mind you, there's unlikelier things than that—you come to me. It may be in my power to 'elp you. And I tell you what you can do for me in exchange. You might take the van 'ome to the stables by yourself, so that I can run round to Rotherhithe New Road and tell my young lady."

"Your young lady!"

"And why not?" demanded William Henry with some indignation. "We ain't all like you."

It gratified Erb, as he parted his hair with an imperfect pocket comb, and tried to make the obstinate wisp at the back of his head remain flat, to think that he had the reputation of one who exhibited no sort of weakness in regard to women; this came in well with his profound attitude towards the world. He had had a letter from the tall upper housemaid at Eaton Square, to which he had sent no reply; indeed, the communication scarcely demanded an answer, for it furnished only information in regard to the weather, and a fervent hope that his health had not been impaired by his presence at the dance; it would not have remained in his memory but for one sentence, "Her young ladyship has spoken of you once or twice." An incomplete way of conveying a fact: something, of course, to know that she had referred to him, but it would have been more interesting to know the precise terms. He flushed at the appalling thought that she might have made some humorous comment on his behaviour.

Men balanced themselves on the edge of the kerb outside the "Druid's Arms," and whilst a swollen faced cornet blared patriotic tunes at them from the opposite side in a ferocious way that permitted of no argument, some of the youngest tried to do a few steps of a dance. Two butchers, affecting to be rivals, chaffed each other derisively in raucous voices, one demanding to know how the widow was, and, on the second man replying incautiously, "What widder?" the first explained that he referred to the widow of the man who bought a joint at the second man's shop last Saturday week. A hoarse voiced man sold cough tablets for the voice; a mild, sightless old man, with bootlaces, had an eager little girl with him, who cried shrilly and commandingly and unceasingly, "Petronise the belind, petronise the belind, petronise the—" Boys and girls thrust bunches of flowers against the noses of passers by; a depressed woman cried, "Twenty four comic papers for a punny," with a catch in her voice that expressed regret at the small demand for humour. Erb nodded to the uniformed men whom he recognised, and, going into the bar, found his competitor Spanswick. Always a short, stout man, Spanswick to night had every sign of his insufficient neck covered with white collar; Erb was pleased to see that Spanswick's tie had rucked up at the back.

Spanswick stopped suddenly in the remarks he was making to an interested group who stood leaning over him in the manner of palm trees, and, coming away, shook hands publicly and elaborately with Erb, as men in the boxing ring salute their opponents.

"Feeling fit?"

"Never better," said Erb. "How's yourself?"

"Bit of a cold," said Spanswick with important reserve; "but otherwise—"

If there is time, one would like to explain here Spanswick's position amongst the men. It was of that assured kind that newcomers do not dare to question, and contemporaries have agreed to respect. If this ever exhibited signs of waning, Spanswick would gather an audience together and beat the bounds of the incident that had made him a man to be treated with consideration, and the story had been re told so many times, and so many improvements and additions had been made to it, that for the sake of true history the real facts may as well be set down.

Spanswick had given way to drink. To say this meant much, for at the time the limits set upon the consumption of beer by many of the carmen was only that fixed by their own capabilities. Spanswick's case must have been exceptional, and, indeed, he was so inclined, not so much to the bottle, perhaps, as to the quart, that his appearance on the morning following these carousals was truly deplorable: his strong minded wife taking these opportunities to damage his face, with the eventual result that his van boy and his horse sneered at him openly. Wherefore Payne and a man named Kirby and another called Old Jim, decided, in the best interests of mankind at large, and of Spanswick in particular, that some steps should be taken, that it was for them to take these steps, and that the following Friday evening (being pay day) was the time to be selected. Payne's idea was this. They would run Spanswick to earth in one of his resorts, they would form a ring (or as much of a ring as three could make) around him, and by wise counsel and urgent illustration force upon him a recognition of the downward career that was his, and its inevitable end. It took some time to arrive at this decision, because Old Jim, who was not abreast of the times and of modern methods, had a remedy that included the dropping of the patient in the canal; whilst Kirby had another proposal. "Let us set the teetotal chaps on him," urged Kirby. Payne's scheme was adopted, and, the Friday night arriving, the three, after they had finished work, had a shave and a wash, and put on their best clothes (Payne himself wore a silk hat of adequate age, but of insufficient size), and they set out solemnly to take up their self appointed duties.

"Now," said Old Jim, "the likeliest place is 'The World Turned Upside Down.'"

"Pardon me," said Kirby, with the politeness that comes with the wearing of Sunday clothes, "pardon me, but 'The Chequers' is his 'ouse."

"I thought," remarked Payne, "the 'Dun Cow' was."

"I'm prutty sure I'm right," said Old Jim.

"I'm jolly well certain you're both wrong," declared Kirby with emphasis.

"Standing here all night arguin'," decided Payne, "won't settle the matter. Let's make a start at one of them."

Spanswick was not in "The World Turned Upside Down," but the three had a drink there, because it would be notoriously a gross breach of etiquette to go from a public house without ordering refreshment; to do this were to deride the landlord openly, and insinuate libels on his stock. At the next place the three went into each bar to make sure, and, having money in their pockets, it seemed like doing the thing well and completely to have a drink here in every bar, still discussing the painful case of poor old Spanny, regretting deeply the curse that liquor brought upon men who could not use it with discretion.

"It's good servant," said Old Jim, raising his glass and shutting one eye in order to see it clearly, "but bad mas'er. That's what I always says about it. It's a good mas'r, but—What I mean to say is it's a bad servant—"

"Every man," declared Kirby, attempting to slap the counter, but missing it, "ought to know where to draw line."

"The chap who don't," agreed Payne, "(You're upsetting your glass, Jim, old man)—the chap who don't is like the beas's of field."

"Worse!" said Old Jim.

"No, not worse!" urged Payne obstinately.

"Fight you for it," offered Old Jim.

Kirby interfered and made peace, and throughout the evening, wherever they went in search of Spanswick, it happened that some two of the three were always quarrelling, whilst the third endeavoured to appease and conciliate. They were on the very edge of a triangular dispute in the last house of call when Payne, sobering himself for a moment, pointed out to the others that it was closing time, and they must not go to bed without feeling that something accomplished, something done, had earned a night's repose; necessary that they should proceed now with as much directness as possible to Spanswick's house, and (if they found him) there deliver the calculated words of warning, the prepared sentences of advice.

"'Ullo, old man," said Payne, as the door of Spanswick's house opened. "Many 'appy returns day."

"What's all this?" demanded Spanswick coldly. "Brought anything with you in a bottle?"

"We've brought good 'dvice," said Old Jim, seating himself on the sill. "How is it we didn't see you at any of the places?"

"The wife locked up me boots," replied Spanswick surlily. "That's why. But surely one of you's got a bottle about him somewheres. Search!"

"We want you, old chap," said Payne, steadying himself with a hand on either side of the doorway, "to give up the drink. 'Oh that man should put an en'my into his mouth to steal out his brains.' Chuck it, my friend, chuck it, before it is too late. Shun the flowing bowl, and save your money to buy harmonium with."

"I'll harmonium you," said Spanswick threateningly, "if you don't all three of you make yourselves precious scarce. How dare you come round here in this disgraceful condition to annoy a sober, honest man? Go to your 'omes and take an example by me. I never saw such a painful exhibition in all me life."

"How was we to know you'd be sober?" asked Kirby, swaying.

Spanswick emphasised the situation by remaining comparatively sober for a week; a busy week in other ways, for he lost no opportunity of reciting the incident of his own pure and heroic action, establishing thus a concrete foundation for the building up of a character that had never entirely disappeared.

(This is the story of carman Spanswick.)

One or two men standing at the zinc bar called on Erb to have a drink, but Erb replied, "Afterwards," and went up the wooden staircase to the club room. There, on the landing, men were consulting in undertones, which they changed for much louder speech on seeing Erb, commencing to talk noisily of contests with superiors whom they had, it appeared, worsted in argument; of fresh young horses that required a somewhat similar treatment; of trouble in regard to Shuts up, to water allowances, to Brought backs, and other technical matters. A late colleague of Erb's introduced him to those who were strangers, and Erb made quite a considerable effort to exhibit friendly manners, until a South Western man, mistaking him for Spanswick, told him some of the things that were being said about young Barnes, whereupon Erb left and went into the club room. In the club room tables had been arranged in something of the shape of a capital U, and at the base a wooden hammer had been placed and a decanter and tumbler; sheets of blue foolscap and scarlet blotting paper gave the room an official, business like appearance. Payne was there in mufti as to coat, in uniform as to waistcoat and corduroy trousers; he was to be proposed as Chairman, and he stood now with his face to a Scotch whisky advertisement, his lips moving silently; he nodded to Erb, and went on with his rehearsal. Spanswick coming up with his entourage, took one of the sheets of paper and, with the stump of a pencil, began to make calculations which were audited, as he went on, by his friends. A few of the men marked the special nature of the proceedings by smoking cigars. The alert clock on the mantelpiece struck the half hour in a sharp, energetic way and hurried on.

"I beg to move that Jack Payne do take the chair."

"I beg to second."

"All in favour," said the first voice. "On the contrary? Carried unanimously and nem. con. Jack" (turning to Mr. Payne), "in you go."

"In ordinary circs," said Payne, after he had taken the chair and had risen to some applause, "I'm perfectly well aware that the proper course to pursue at an affair like this is for the chair to call on the secretary to read the minutes of the last meeting. I know that without any of you telling me. But we're in the position to night of not 'aving no secretary and not 'aving no previous meetin'."

The heads around the table nodded agreement. A gloomy man seated in the position that a vice chairman might have occupied half rose and said, "Mr. Chairman, sir," and was at once pulled back into his chair by those near him.

"I was never a man," went on the Chairman, his forehead damp with nervousness, "to what you may call force me opinions on any body of men. 'Cepting once, and that was at New Cross in '89. I forget exactly what it was about, and I forget who was there, and I forget what I said, but the entire incident is quite fresh in my memory, and, as I say, that was the only occasion on which—"

"Question, question," cried the gloomy man at the other end of the room. His neighbours hushed him into silence.

"I'm coming to the question as fast as ever I can. Few know better than me how to conduct a meeting of this kind, although I say it p'raps as shouldn't, because it sounds like flattery, but it ain't flattery, it's only the truth. I've had it said to me over and over again, not once or twice, but many times—"

"Mr. Chairman, reely," said the gloomy man, "I must call you to order. We shall never get the business done this side of Chris'mas if—"

"Kindly sed down," ordered Mr. Payne, in tones of command, "or else resume your seat; one or the other. It's me," tapping his waistcoat, "me, sir, that calls people to order, not you."

The gloomy man argued in a loud whisper with his neighbours, and, on these counselling that he should simmer down, sat back in his chair, surveying the ceiling, his lips closed determinedly.

"First thing is shall we, being all of a trade, form a separate society, or shall we jolly well do the other thing? That's the point. Now then, who's going to give us a start? You, my friend, of the Great Eastern, down at the bottom of this left 'and table, you seem to have a lot to say, p'raps we might give you ten minutes and see whether or not there's any sense in you."

The gloomy man affected deafness until this had been explained to him by those sitting near, on which he told them rather haughtily that he spoke when he liked, and not when he was called upon.

"Then we must throw the 'andkerchief to somebody else. Spanswick, you might set the ball a rolling. Don't be longer than you can 'elp."

Erb watched. The impression that his rival made now would affect the later decision, and Erb could not help wishing that Spanswick might prove halting in utterance and clumsy of speech. Cheers greeted Spanswick; some of the men looked at Erb, as they slapped the table with the palms of their hands to see how he took it, and Erb remembered, just in time, to join in the compliment. He recovered his hopefulness as soon as Spanswick spoke, for he noted that his opponent started with great rapidity of utterance, speaking also overloudly—encouraging facts both. Spanswick was, of course, urging that they should form a separate society, but he had no arguments, only hurried expressions of his own opinion. Erb, with his eyes on a sheet of foolscap paper, noticed that the room relaxed its attention; the gloomy man had his watch out, and was clearly preparing to shout at the appropriate moment, "Time, time!" Spanswick halted and went over one sentence twice, word for word. Then he stopped altogether, and the silent room saw him endeavour to recall his fleeting memory, saw him take from the inside pocket of his coat the entire speech and laboriously find the place.

"Beg pardon," cried the gloomy man, starting up, "but is a member entitled to read—"

Spanswick, with now and again an anxious glance at Erb, read the remainder of his speech in a shamed undertone. There was but little cheering when he finished; he was called up again because he had forgotten to move the resolution. Four men competed for the honour of seconding this.

"Now then!" said the Chairman, with relish, "let's go on in a orderly manner. First thing is, any amendment? No amendment? Vurry well, then! Now, is there any further remarks? The subject hasn't been, if I may say so, thor'ly threshed out yet, and if—Thank you! Friend Barnes will now address the meeting."

Erb rose with the slight nervousness that he always felt in commencing a speech. He began slowly and quietly: the Great Eastern man saw his chance for an interruption, and shouted, "Let's 'ear you," but Erb took no notice. They were there, he said, to inaugurate a great work, a work to which some of them had given a considerable amount of care, and the scheme was so far advanced that he thought he could place a few details before them for consideration. There had been the grave question whether they should join the general society of London carmen, or whether they should form an independent society of their own.

"On a point of order, sir—" began the gloomy man.

"If there is one man," said Erb, raising his voice, "in this room who is absolutely ignorant of order it is our Great Eastern friend at the other end of the room. A yelping little terrier that runs after a van doesn't make the van go faster."

The room, now very crowded with uniformed men, especially near the doorway, approved this, and the Great Eastern man first looked round for support from his own colleagues, and, obtaining none, began to take desperate notes as Erb went on.

"I can't waste time over a man who can only interrupt: I address myself to you. First, let me put my friend Spanswick right on a small detail. He urged that we should work quietly and secretly"—(cheers from Spanswick's supporters)—"I disagree! I fail to see the usefulness of that. I think that all we do should be fair and above board, and I say this because if you combine, and let the railway companies see that you are combining, you will be treated with greater respect. See what's happened in the case of my own late fellow carmen! It's true I was sacrificed, but let that pass; see what advantages they got, just for the asking. They got—"

Payne's watch must have been suddenly affected, for he allowed Erb to speak for more than the period of ten minutes; no one complained; they were all too much interested. When Erb, in a fiery peroration, appealed to them to extend the recent action and make it general, with a strong reference to individualism, which they did not understand, and about which Erb himself was not quite sure, then the supporters of Spanswick forgot their reticence and cheered with the rest.

"And I trust," added Erb modestly and finally, "that I 'aven't took up too much of your time."

The resolution was carried.

"Now," said the Chair, "if any of you thought of standing me a drink, or even of 'aving one yourself, p'raps you'll seize the opportunity whilst the waiters are in the room, and then we can shut them out whilst we go on to the next bisness."

"Erb!" cried Spanswick along the table, "what's yours?"

It was felt that this was a great piece of strategy on Spanswick's part, and Erb's refusal counted nothing for righteousness; one or two of Erb's supporters shook their heads to intimate that this was not diplomacy. The waiters brought in japanned trays of glasses on their high, outstretched palms, carrying change everywhere, in their pockets, in their tweed caps, in a knot in their handkerchiefs, in their mouths. They completed their work in a few minutes and went, obeying leisurely the Chairman's imperious wave of the hammer.

"We come, now," said Payne loudly, "to what I venture to term the principal item on the agender. That is, the appointment of secretary." Both Erb and Spanswick showed signs of puzzled astonishment. "There's no less than two suggestions that have been 'anded up: one is that we should 'ave a honery secretary, which I may explain for the benefit of some, means one who will perform his services in a honery way: the other is that we should 'ave a paid secretary, which means that we should have to plank down about a 'undred a year, otherwise, two quid a week, and that'd cover his slight travelling expenses. There's a good deal," added the Chair impartially, "to be said on both sides, and, at this stage of the proceedings, I don't attempt to dictate. This room's a bit warmish, and if you don't mind me taking off my coat, why, I shall be more comfortable than what I am at the present moment."

The men around the table imitated example, and, hanging their jackets on the backs of the chairs, addressed themselves to the new subject.

"What?" said the Chair. "You woke up again?"

"I should like to ask," said the gloomy Great Eastern man, ignoring this remark, "whether there's any sense in paying a 'undred pounds a year for a article that we can get for nothing? That's all I want to know."

"Argue the point, my good sir," urged the Chair, "argue in a speech."

"I've said my say," retorted the other stubbornly.

"If it was the self same article," said the Chair, shaking his hammer in a friendly way towards the Great Eastern man, "then I should be with you. But is it?" The shirt sleeves rested on the tables; the men began to show renewed interest.

"I asked a plain question, I want a plain answer!"

"Oh!" said the Chair, disgustedly, "you go to—well, I won't say where. You've got no more idea of conducting a meeting than this 'ammer. Why don't someone prepose a resolution?"

"Beg—propose," said a young man desperately, "my friend Spanswick—honery sec'tary—new society."

"Beg second that," jerked another youth.

"In view of the fac'," said a South Eastern man, half rising, "that if you want a thing done well you ought to pay for it, I think we ought to 'ave a man who'll devote his whole energies to the work. Therefore, I beg to suggest Erb Barnes as—as—"

"Organisin' secretary!" whispered a neighbour.

"I second that vote—mean to say, resolution."

"Any other names?" asked the Chair. "Very good then! Now, I shall ask these two chaps to kindly retire, in other words, to leave the room, so as to leave us free to discuss—"

"Point of order occurs to me," interrupted the gloomy Great Eastern man acutely, "Can they leave the room?"

The room watched Erb and Spanswick as the two made their way behind the chairs to the doorway. Erb opened the door, and motioned to Spanswick to go first, but Spanswick, not to be outdone in politeness, declined absolutely, insisting that Erb should take precedence, and when they decided to stop the display of courtesy, both blundered out at the same moment. As they closed the door behind them they heard several voices addressing the chair.

"Ever gone in for scarlet runners?" asked Spanswick. "I've only got a little bit of a garden, but I suppose there isn't another man in Rotherhithe that grows the scarlet runners I do; people come from far and near to see 'em. There's a good deal of art, mind you, in the stickin' of 'em. Sunflowers, too! I've had tremendous luck with my sunflowers. I believe I could grow most anything in my little back place if it wasn't for the cats. Vurry good plan of dealin' with cats—"

Erb allowed his rival to make conversation whilst he himself considered the importance of these moments that were passing. He looked hard at a picture on the walls of the landing, a picture representing a cheerful Swiss valley and advertising Somebody's Ginger Beer; the villagers held goblets containing (presumably) this beverage, and toasted the snow topped mountains at the back. He forced himself to recognise that his chances were small; unless he had made a particularly good impression by his speech he had no chance at all; he would have to commence to morrow morning a round of calls on master carmen and on contracting firms with the obsequious inquiry, "You don't 'appen to want a hand, I s'pose?" and receiving the negative reply. He had obtained a clean character from the Railway Company, and the Chief had wished him good luck, but the information that he was a stirabout would fly round in advance of him, and all the best places would be on the defensive. It might come to driving a cheap coal van, otherwise known as working in the slate business. There was an alternative even less agreeable to think of. He knew one or two men who had just missed being leaders of labour, who sometimes opened debates at Clubs, and were paid fairly liberal expenses, who were sometimes approached by the capitalists to stump through London in an endeavour to lash working men into a state of indignation in regard to Foreign Competition, Sugar Bounties, or the tyranny of Trades Unions, or some other subject for which the capitalists had affection: these men at times coalesced and, urged by a common jealousy, denounced some prominent men of their own party, and found their names mentioned in the opposition journals, the reporters of which bribed them in order to obtain exclusive information of semi public meetings. Erb told the Swiss valley that it would be long ere he came down to that.

"You take a spade," exclaimed his companion, "an ornery spade will do, and you dig it in the garden like so, and what do you find? Why you find—"

Young Louisa would be disappointed too. Louisa had been less successful since the servants' dance at Eaton Square in cloaking her admiration for her brother, and the last young man had been dismissed with ignominy because he showed hesitation in sacrificing his own views on political subjects and accepting those held by Erb. If he had not already passed from the memory of Lady Frances, she might perhaps inquire of Alice the result of the meeting, and, hearing it, would smile agreeably and push him away from her thoughts. To be shown through Bermondsey by an official in the labour world would be one thing; to be conducted by a grimy faced carman was another. And there was Rosalind—Rosalind—what was her other name?

"Now, in regard to meenure," said Spanswick dogmatically, "the long and short of the matter is simply this."

He had found in Southampton Street, Camberwell, on the previous day (being on the Surrey side round), a painted board on a house announcing here, "Elocution and Public Speaking Taught! Pupils prepared for the Dramatic Stage! Apply within to Professor Danks!" and it then occurred to him that this was the address given him by the footman in Eaton Square. The front garden was filled with monumental statues belonging to an undertaker next door, and engraved with names and dates, tombstones which for some inexplicable reason had not been used. He had gone up the uneven pavement from the front gate to the door and had knocked there, but the door being opened by the tall, bright eyed girl, plainly and economically dressed, and with a suggestion of care near to her bright eyes, he had for some extraordinary reason, muttered "Beg pardon. Wrong number!" and had stumbled back to the gate, hot faced with confusion. He knew that his powers of speech lacked refinement, and one or two finishing lessons would work miracles: he might perhaps learn how to aspirate without the show of pain and anxiety that he exhibited now when he endeavoured to observe the trying rule. The bright eyed girl, he remembered, had stood at the doorway looking after him rather reproachfully.

"Of course," said the injured voice of Spanswick, "if it's too much trouble for you to listen, why it isn't any use me talking."

"Sorry," he said absently. "Fact is, I don't take very much interest in gardening."

"I was talking about poultry."

"They both come under the same head," remarked Erb.

"I suppose, as a matter of fact, you're pretty keen on this 'ere job?"

"They're a long time deciding," said Erb.

"I've been expectin'," Spanswick made circles on the landing with his right foot in a hesitating way, "I've been expectin' that you'd approach me and ask me to withdraw from the contest."

"What'd be the use of that?"

"Well," said Spanswick in a mysterious whisper, "you know what Shakespeare says?"

"He said a lot."

"You're a mere kid in these matters," remarked the other contemptuously, walking away to the other end of the landing. "Haven't you never 'eard of buying off the opposition? In the present case, suppose you was to say, 'Spanny, old man, is twen'y five bob any use to you?' and I should answer 'Well, I could do with it,' and you paid the money over 'ere." Spanswick held out one hand. "And I said, 'Well, now, come to think of it, what's the good of this job to me? I shan't make nothing out of it, unless it is a silver teapot for the missus; I'll withdraw my nomination and leave you a clear field.' See?"

"Upon my word," exclaimed Erb indignantly, "upon my word if you ain't the biggest—"

"Mind you," interrupted the other, "I was only putting a suppositious case." The door of the club room opened, and a voice said importantly, "Spanswick and Barnes, this way, please." They turned to obey. "There y'are," said Spanswick reproachfully, "you've left it too late."

Looking over the banisters, Erb saw that women folk had arrived, charged with the double duty of listening to the coming concert and of conveying their male relatives home at a reasonable hour. Louisa's white young face glanced up at him with a twitch, and asked anxiously whether it was all over; Erb replied that, on the contrary, it was just about to begin.

"Kindly take your former seats," said the Chairman importantly. The chattering room became quiet as the two men entered, and Payne rapped with his hammer for silence. "The voting has come out," he went on, looking at some figures on the sheet of foolscap before him, "the voting has come out 29 on one side and 14 on the other."

The rattle of conversation recommenced.

"Less noise there, less noise!" cried the Chair urgently. "I can't 'ear meself talk."

"Wish we couldn't," remarked the Great Eastern man from his end of the table.

"Be careful, my friend," said the Chair warningly. "Be careful, or else I shall rule you out of order. I have the pleasure now of calling on my friend Erb Barnes." The room cheered. "Order, please, for Erb Barnes."

"What have I got to talk about?" demanded Erb.

"Talk about?" echoed the Chair amazedly. "Talk about? Why, you've got to acknowledge in a few appropriate words your appointment as paid organisin' secretary of the Railway Carmen's Society."

CHAPTER V

Erb entered upon his duties with appetite. The single office of the new society was a spare room over a coffee tavern in Grange Road, and the first disbursement was for the painting on the window in bold white letters the full title of the society, with the added words, "Herbert Barnes, secretary." (Young Louisa went five minutes out of her way, morning and evening, in order to see this proclamation of her brother's name.) To the office came Erb promptly every morning at an hour when the attendants at the coffee room were on their knees scrubbing, chairs set high on tables, and forms on end against the walls, and the young women were a good deal annoyed by the fact that Erb, in these circumstances, bestowed on them none of the chaff and badinage which were as necessary to their existence as the very air. When he had gone through the post letters—the more there were of these the more contented he was—and had answered them on post cards, he went out, fixing a notice on the door, "Back Shortly. Any messages leave at Bar," and hurried to some railway depot, or some point where railway carmen were likely to congregate, hurrying non members into becoming members, passing the word round in regard to public meetings, hunting for grievances, and listening always, even when some, with erroneous ideas of his duties, requested advice in regard to some domestic trouble with lodgers, or insubordination on the part of babes. All this meant visits to Paddington, to Willesden, to Dalston, to Poplar, to Nine Elms: it gave to him a fine sensation of ruling London and, in some way, the thought that he was repairing errors made by the Creator of the world. He came in contact with the white haired Labour member of Parliament, and watched his manner closely; the Labour member invited Erb one evening to the House of Commons, and Erb found that the Labour member had for the House a style differing entirely from that which he used in other places, measuring words with care, speaking with deliberation, and avoiding all the colloquialisms and the jagged sentences that made him popular when he addressed outdoor meetings. And as all young men starting the journey through life model themselves on some one who has arrived, Erb determined to acquire this admirable alternative manner.

Thus it was that one Thursday evening he took courage by the hand, and went Camberwell way to call again at the house where on his previous visit he had made undignified departure because of a pair of rather bright eyes. He thought of her with some nervousness as he went down Camberwell New Road, and, putting aside for a moment the serious matters, gave himself the joy of reviewing his female acquaintances. He had just come to the sage decision that different women exacted entirely different tributes, some demanding reverence, others admiration, and others something more fervent, when he found himself at the gate and the uneven path between the monumental statuary that led to the door of Professor Danks's house. The street was one affecting to make a short cut to Queen's Road, Peckham, but it did not really make a short cut; within its crescent form it included new model dwellings of a violent red, elderly houses with red verandahs, a Liberal Club, and a chapel. A part of the road had undergone the process of being shopped, which is to say that the long useless front gardens had been utilised, and anxious, empty, unsuccessful young establishments came out to the pavement, expending all their profits on gas, and making determined efforts either by placard or minatory signs to persuade the passers by that business was enormous, and that it was with difficulty that customers could be checked in their desire to patronise. One had started with the proud boast, "Everything at Sixpence halfpenny," and had later altered the six to five, and the five to four; only necessary to allow time, and there seemed some good prospect that the reckless shop would eventually give its contents free. Erb pulled at the bell handle, and it came out obligingly.

"Now you 'ave gone and done it," said the small servant who opened the door. "That's clever, that is. I suppose you get medals for doing tricks like that? Well, well," she continued fractiously, as Erb made no reply, "don't stand there like a great gawk with the knob in your 'and. What d'you want?"

"Might Professor Danks be in?" asked Erb.

"He might and he might not," explained the small servant. "He's jest sleepin' it off a bit on the sofa."

"Can I see anyone else?"

"Come in," said the girl with a burst of friendliness. "Never mind about wipin' your boots; it's getting to the end of the week. You could see her if you didn't mind waiting till she's finished giving a lesson."

"Shall I wait here in the passage?"

"Don't disturb him," whispered the girl, "if I let you rest your weary bones in the back room." She opened the door of the back room quietly. "She's as right as rain," whispered the girl confidently, "but he—" The girl gave an expressive wave of the hand, signifying that the Professor was not indispensable to the world's happiness. Erb went in. "I'd stay and chat to you," she said through the doorway, "only there's my ironin'. I've got the 'ole 'ouse to look after, mind you, besides answering the front door."

"Takes a bit of doing, no doubt."

"You never said a truer word," whispered the short servant. "There's pictures in that magazine you can look at. If you want me, 'oller 'Lizer!' over the banisters."

Professor Danks, asleep on the sofa, had the Era over his face for better detachment from a wakeful world: the paper was slipping gradually, and Erb, watching him over the top of the book, knew that the eclipse would be over and the features fully visible in a few minutes. Meanwhile, he noticed that the Professor was a large, heavy man, with snowy hair at one end, and slippers which had walked along muddy pavements at the other; not a man, apparently, of active habits.

"I fear I shall never make anything of you," her decided voice came from the front room. "You don't pay attention. You don't seem to remember what I tell you."

"Mustn't be too harsh with my husband, miss," said a voice with the South London whine. "We all have to make a beginning, don't forget that."

"Now, sir. Once more, please, we'll go through this piece of poetry. And when you say the first lines, 'Give others the flags of foreign states,' show some animation; don't say the words casually, as though you were talking of the weather."

"You understand, miss," interposed the pupil's wife, "that he's made up the words out of his own head."

"I am sure of that," with a touch of sarcasm.

"But, whilst he's very clever in putting poetry together, he is not so good—I'm speaking, Albert dear, for your own benefit—he is not so good in reciting of them. And we go out into Society a great deal (there's two parties on at New Cross only next month that we're asked to), and what I thought was that it would be so nice any time when an evening began to go a bit slow for me to say casually, ye know, 'Albert, what about that piece you made up yourself?' Then for him to get up and recite it in a gentlemanly way."

"Come now," said the instructress, "'Give others the flags of foreign states, I care not for them a jot.'"

"Of course," interposed the wife again, "his high pitched voice is against him, but that's his misfortune, not his fault. Also you may think that he's left it rather late to take up with elocution. If we'd ever had any children of our own—"

"I really think," said the girl, "that we must get on with the lesson. Now, sir, if you please. 'Give others the flags.'"

The Era had slipped from the Professor's red face, and the swollen, poached egg eyes moved, the heavy eyelids made one or two reluctant efforts to unclose. The room, Erb thought, looked as though it were troubled by opposing forces, one anxious to keep it neat and keep it comfortable, the other with entirely different views, and baulking these efforts with some success. Erb saw the household clearly and felt a desire to range himself on the side of order.

"Good evening," he said, when the leaden eyelids had decided to open. "Having your little nap, sir?"

The Professor sat up, kneading his eyes and then rubbing his white hair violently.

"I have been," he said, in a voice that would have sounded important if it had not been hoarse, "making a brief excursion into the land of dreams." He clicked his tongue. "And a devil of a mouth I've got on me, too." He rose heavily and went to a bamboo table where two syphons were standing, tried them, and found they were empty. "A curse," he said, "on both your houses."

"I've called about some lessons."

"Lessons!" repeated the Professor moodily. "That I, Reginald Danks, should be reduced to this! I, who might have been at the Lyceum at the present moment but for fate and Irving. How many lessons," he asked with a change of manner, "do you require, laddie?"

"I thought about six," said Erb.

"Make it a dozen. We offer thirteen for the price of twelve."

"What would that number run me into? I want them more for public speaking than anything else."

"We shall do the whole bag of tricks for you," said the Professor, placing an enormous hand on Erb's shoulder, "for a mere trifle."

"Who is 'we?'"

"Rather should you say, 'To whom is it that you refer?' In this self appointed task of imparting the principles of voice production and elocution to the—to the masses," the Professor seemed to restrain himself forcibly from using a contumelious adjective, "I have the advantage of valuable assistance from my daughter. Her system is my system, her methods are my methods, her rules are my rules. If at any time I should be called away on professional business," here the Professor passed his hand over his lip, "my daughter, Rosalind, takes my place. What is your age?"

Erb gave the information.

"Ah," the Professor sighed deeply, "in '74 I was with Barry Sullivan doing the principal towns in a repertoire. No, I'm telling you a lie. It was not in '74. It was in the autumn of '73. I played Rosencrantz and the First Grave digger—an enormous success."

"Which?"

"I went from Barry Sullivan to join the 'Murderous Moment' Company, and that," said the Professor, striking his waistcoat, "was perhaps one of the biggest triumphs ever witnessed on the dramatic stage. From that hour, sir, from that hour I never looked back."

The high voiced pupil in the front room finished his lesson, and his wife took him off with the congratulatory remark that he promised well to make her relatives at forthcoming parties sit up with astonishment. The Professor's daughter, seeing them both to the front door, remarked that her pupil would be able to find his way alone the next time, whereupon the pupil's wife answered darkly, "Do you really think I should let him go out?"

"Shall I settle with you?" asked Erb.

"My daughter Rosalind," said the Professor regretfully, "insists, as a general rule, on taking charge of the business side, but on this occasion—"

"If that's the rule," interrupted Erb, "don't let's break it. I don't want any misunderstanding about matters of cash."

"There have been times in my life, sir, when money has been as nothing to me. Will you believe that there was a time in my professional career when I earnt twenty guineas—twenty of the best—per week?"

"Since you ask me, my answer is 'No.'"

"You are quite right," said the Professor, and in no way disconcerted. "Let us be exact in our statements or perish. Not twenty guineas, twenty pounds. But that," he went on rather hurriedly, "that was at a time when real acting, sir, was appreciated. Nowadays they walk in from the streets. Ee locution is a lost art; acting, real acting, is not to be seen on the London boards. If you have a cigarette about you, I can get a light from the fireplace."

Erb acted upon this hint, and listened for the girl's voice.

"Her mother," went on the Professor, puffing at the cigarette, and then looking at it disparagingly, "her mother before she fell ill—mind, I'm not complaining—was perhaps, without exception, the most diversified arteest that ever graced the dramatic stage. Ingénue, old woman, soubrette, nothing came amiss to her. That was the difference between us—she liked work. And when, just before the end, when I'd been out of engagement for some time, she had an offer for the pair of us, two pounds ten the couple, such was her indomitable spirit that she actually wanted to accept it. But I said 'No.' I put my foot down. I admit," said the Professor genially, "that I lost my temper with her. I told her pretty definitely that I had made up my mind—"

"Your what?" inquired Erb.

"That poverty I could face, dee privation I could endure, hunger and thirst I could welcome with o pen arms, but a contemptuous proposition such as this I could not, should not, and would not tolerate. I repeated this," added the Professor with a fine roll and a sweep of the left hand, "at the inquest."

"You're a nice one, I don't think," said Erb critically. "How is it they let you live on?"

"Laddie," said the Professor, tearfully, "my life is not an enviable one even now. My own daughter—Soft!—she comes."

It occurred to Erb later that in his anxiety to show himself a careless, self possessed fellow, he rather overdid it, presenting himself in the light of one slightly demented. He nodded his head on formal introduction by the Professor, hummed a cheerful air, and, taking out a packet of cigarette papers, blew at one, and recollecting, twisted the detached slip into a butterfly shape and puffed it to the ceiling. The girl looked at him, at her father, then again at Erb. She had a pencil resting between the buttons of her pink blouse, and but for a slight contraction of the forehead that is the public sign of private worry, would have been a very happy looking young person indeed.

"A would be student," said her father with a proud wave of the hand towards Erb, as though he had just made him, "a would be student, my love: one anxious to gain at our hands the principles of voice pro duction and ee locution."

"When do you propose to begin, sir?" she asked, limping slightly as she went to a desk.

"Soon as your father's ready, miss."

"I have heard you speak in the park."

"Most people have!" replied Erb, with a fine assumption of indifference.

"I'll just register your name, please."

"Our sys tem," said the Professor oracularly, as Erb bent over her and gave the information (there was a pleasant warm scent from her hair), "is to conduct everything in a perfectly businesslike manner. I remember on one occasion Mr. Phelps said to me, 'Danks, my dear young friend, never, never—' My dear Rosalind, give me the word. What was it," the Professor tapped his large forehead reprovingly, "what was it I was talking about?"

"I don't think it matters, father. You pay in advance, please," she said to Erb. "Thank you. I'm not sure that I have sufficient change in the house."

"I will step down the road," suggested the Professor with a slight excess of eagerness, "and obtain the necessary—"

"No, father."

"Think I've got just enough silver," said Erb.

"Thank you, Mr. Barnes."

Good to be called Mister, better still to find it accompanied by a smile of gratitude that somehow also intimated comradeship and a defensive alliance against the ingenious Professor. The Professor, affecting to examine a pimple on his chin at the mirror, looked at his daughter's reflection in an appealing way; but she shook her head quickly. The Professor sighed and, turning back the cuffs of his shirt, put on an elderly velvet jacket.

"I have some work to do downstairs," she said, with a curt little bow to Erb. "You will excuse me."

"Only too pleased, miss," he said blunderingly.

"Father, you will give Mr. Barnes an hour, please, in the front room. I will come up when the time is—"

"Then I needn't say good bye," remarked Erb gallantly.

The Professor in the front room declaimed to the new pupil a passage from the "Merchant of Venice," from the centre of the carpet, and then invited him to repeat it, which Erb did, the Professor arresting him at every line, correcting the accent with acerbity and calling attention to the aspirates with something like tears. "Why don't you speak naturally, sir?" demanded the Professor, hitting his own chest with his fist, "as I dew?" At the end of twenty minutes, when the Professor had furnished some really valuable rules in regard to the artifices of voice production, he gave a sudden dramatic start, and begged Erb for pity's sake not to tell him that the day was Thursday and the hour half past seven. On Erb admitting his inability to give him other information without stepping beyond the confines of truth, the Professor strode up and down the worn carpet in a state of great agitation, declaring that unless he were in the Strand by eight fifteen, or, at the very latest, eight twenty that evening, he would, in all probability, lose the chance of a lifetime.

"What am I to do?" he asked imploringly. "I appeal to you, laddie? Show me where duty calls?"

On Erb suggesting that perhaps Miss Rosalind would finish the lesson, the Professor shook him warmly by both hands and ordered heaven in a dictatorial way to rain down blessings on the head of his pupil. One difficulty remained. Time pressed, and every moment was (in all probability) golden. Could Mr. Barnes, as an old friend, oblige with half a—no, not half a crown, two shillings. The Professor, in the goodness of his heart, did not mind four sixpences, and hurrying out into the passage, struggled into a long brown overcoat of the old Newmarket shape, took his soft hat, and, having called over the banisters to his daughter to favour him with a moment's conversation, bustled through the passage whispering to Erb, "You can explain better than I," and going out, closed the door quietly. There were signs of flour on the girl's plump arms as she came up; she rolled down the sleeves of the pink blouse as she entered the front room. Her forehead contracted as she listened.

"How much did he borrow?" she asked, checking a sigh.

"Nothing," replied Erb boldly.

"Two shillings or a half a crown?"

"But I couldn't possibly think for a moment—" he began protestingly.

"I wish you had," she said. "Take it, please. I don't want father to run into debt if I can help it."

"Makes me feel as though I'm robbing you."

"Do you know," said Miss Rosalind, with not quite half a smile, "it makes me feel as though I were being robbed. Let us get on with the lesson, please; I have another pupil coming at half past eight." Erb, for a hot moment, was consumed with unreasonable jealousy of the next pupil. "She is always punctual," added Rosalind, and Erb became cooler. "Take this book, please, and read aloud the passage I have marked."

There were faded photographs on the mantelpiece of ladies with exuberant smiles, calculated to disarm any criticism in regard to their eccentric attire, their signatures sprawled across the lower right hand corner, "Ever yours most affectionate!" A frame that had seen stormy days outside provincial theatres hung on the wall with the address of its last exhibition half rubbed off. Erb as he listened to the girl's serious corrections and warning, guessed that the half dozen portraits it contained were all of Rosalind's mother; they ranged from one as Robinson Crusoe with a white muff to a more matronly representation of (judging from her hat) a designing Frenchwoman holding a revolver in one hand, and clearly prepared to use this. In another she was fondling a child, whose head and face were almost covered by a stage wig, and the child bore some far away resemblance to the present instructress. On Rosalind limping across the room to place on the fire an economical lump of coal, Erb framed an expression of sympathy; common sense most fortunately gagged him.

"You left school when you were very young?" said the girl, looking over her shoulder from the fireplace.

"Pawsed the sixth standard when I was—"

"Oh, please, please! Don't say pawsed."

"I passed the sixth standard when I was twelve, because I had to. Father was Kentish born, mother wasn't. Both died in the"—Rosalind put her hands apprehensively to her ears—"in the hospital in one week, both in one week, and I had to set to and get shot of the Board School and go out."

"As?" she asked curiously.

"As chief of the Transport Department to the principal railway companies," said Erb glibly, "and personal friend, and, I may say, adviser to his Royal—"

"We will proceed," said Rosalind, haughty on the receipt of sarcasm, "with the lesson, please. There is much to be done in the way of eradicating errors in your speech."

The reliable lady pupil due at eight thirty spoilt her record by arriving half an hour late. Thus, when Erb's lesson was finished and the clock on the mantelpiece gave the hour in a hurried asthmatic way, there was still time for polite conversation on a variety of topics; the house, Erb discovered, was not theirs, they only occupied furnished apartments; they had lived in many parts of London, because, said Rosalind cautiously, the Professor liked a change now and again. Erb backed slowly towards the door as each subject was discussed, anxious to stay as long as possible, but more anxious still to make his exit with some clever impressive final remark. He found her book of notices, and insisted politely on reading the neatly pasted slips cut from the "Hornsey Express," the "South London Journal," the "Paddington Magpie," and other newspapers of repute, which said "Miss Rosalind Danks in her recitals made the hit of the evening, and the same may be said of all the other artists on the programme." That "Miss R. Danks, as our advertisement column shows, is to give An Evening with the Poets and Humorists at our Town Hall on Thursday evening. We wish her a bumper." That "Miss Rosalind Danks's naïveté of manner and general chic enabled her in an American contribution to score a terrific 'succés d'estime.' She narrowly escaped an enthusiastic encore." That "Miss Danks lacks some of the charms necessary for a good platform appearance—"

"I'd like to argue the point with the man who wrote that," said Erb.

"They have to fill the paper with something," remarked Miss Rosalind.

"For a good platform appearance, but she has a remarkably distinct enunciation, and some of her lines could be heard almost distinctly at the back of the hall." That "Miss Danks comes of a theatrical stock, and her father is none other than the celebrated Mr. Reginald Danks, whose Antonio still remains in the memory of the few privileged to witness it. Mr. Reginald Danks informs us that he has had several offers from West End theatres, but that he has some idea of going in for management himself as soon as a convenient playhouse can be secured. Of this, more anon."

It was natural when Erb had looked through these notices that he should find in his pocket two or three copies of a small poster advertising a lecture by him on the forthcoming Sunday evening, at a hall in Walworth Road. "Mr. Herbert Barnes," said the poster loudly, adding in a lower voice, "Organising Secretary Railway Carmen's Union, will speak on The Working Man: What Will Become of Him? No collection. Discussion invited." Erb gave Miss Rosalind one of these as a present, and then said, "Well now, I must be off," as though he had been detained greatly against his will.

And here it was that Erb made one of those mistakes of commission which the most reliable of us effect at uncertain intervals. He took up the photograph of a fur coated young man, clean shaven face, thin lips, and not quite enough of chin.

"And who," asked Erb pityingly, "who might this young toff be?"

"He is stage manager," she said rather proudly, "to a company touring in the provinces. Plays too."

"Relation?"

"Not yet," said Rosalind.

As Erb blundered through the passage Rosalind warned him to attend to the home work she had given him to do, and to come promptly to his next lesson; she held the door open until Erb went out of the gate, a new politeness which he acknowledged by lifting his hat. He had never lifted his hat to a lady before, and had always smiled contemptuously when he had seen gallant youths performing this act of respect. To atone for this retrograde movement he ran against the tardily arriving lady pupil, and went on without apology. The lady pupil ejaculated, "Clown!" and Erb felt that he had righted himself in his own estimation.

He looked about him as he walked up the crowded pavement towards the Elephant and Castle, because it was always one of his duties to recognise the railway vans. Disappointment clouded his eyes: he blamed himself for so far forgetting the principal duty of his life as to waste time on unremunerative investments. This was why he missed a Brighton goods van standing with its pair of horses near a large shop in Newington Causeway; the van boy reported Erb's negligence to his mate when he returned, and this coming on the top of other annoying circumstances, the Brighton man said to himself, "This shall be chalked up against you, young Erb."

Erb reached Page's Walk, having tried ineffectually to walk himself into a good humour, and found Louisa with a round spot of colour high up on either cheek, looking out of the window of the model dwellings and hailing him excitedly.

"Put that 'ead of yours in," he counselled. "You'll go and catch cold."

"You won't catch much," retorted Louisa, "if you don't arrange to be on 'and when wanted. 'Urry upstairs, I've got something to tell you that can't be bawled."

Erb ran up the stone stairs, and Louisa met him at the door of the sitting room, her eyes bigger than ever with the importance. The room had a slight perfume of violets.

"Who d'you think's been 'ere?"

"Tell us," said Erb.

"But guess," begged Louisa, enjoying the power that was hers.

"Can't guess."

"Lady Frances," said Louisa, in an impressive whisper.

"Well," remarked Erb curtly, "what of it?"

"What of it? Why, she wanted you to show her over Bermondsey, and she waited here upwards of a hower, chatting away to me like anything."

"Any other news?"

"Yes," said Louisa reluctantly, "but nothing of much importance. Letter from Aunt Emma; she's coming up soon. Oh, and a man called to say there was trouble brewin' at Willer Walk, and would you see about it as soon as possible."

"Now," remarked Erb elatedly, "now you're talking."

CHAPTER VI

The particular blend of trouble which Willow Walk was occupied in brewing proved highly attractive to Erb, and one that gave to all the men concerned a taste of the joys that must have come in the French Revolution. A few impetuous young spirits who had been brooding on grievances since the days when they were van boys were responsible. Erb recognised that here was the first opportunity of justifying his appointment. Warned, however, by the example of other organisers within memory, who had sometimes in similar experiments shown a tendency to excess, Erb took care. He wrote letters to the General Manager, letters for which he received a printed form of acknowledgment and no other, he wrote to the Directors, and received a brief reply to the effect that they could not recognise Mr. Herbert Barnes in the matter, and that the grievances of the staff concerned only the staff and themselves; the men were bitterly annoyed at this, but Erb, because he had anticipated the reply, showed no concern. He worked from dawn near to dawn again, sending letters to members of Parliament, going round to the depots of other railways, attending meetings, and in many ways devoting himself to the work of what he called directing public opinion. In point of fact, he had first to create it. For a good fortnight he gave up everything to devote himself to this one object, gave up everything but his lessons in Camberwell. One of the halfpenny evening papers said, amongst other things, "Mr. Herbert Barnes made an impassioned but logical and excellently delivered speech." Erb knew the deplorable looking man with a silk hat of the early seventies who had reported this, but that did not prevent him from being highly gratified on seeing the words in print; Louisa spent eighteenpence on a well bound manuscript book, and in it commenced to paste these notices. The point at issue being that the men demanded better payment of overtime, Erb found here a subject that lent itself to oratorical argument; the story of the man who was so seldom at home that one Sunday his little girl asked the other parent, "Mother, who's this strange man?" never failed to prove effective, and Erb felt justified in leaving out the fact that the carman in question was one accustomed, when his work finished at night, to go straight from the stables to a house in Old Kent Road, where he usually remained until the potman cried "Time! gentlemen, time!"

The men had sent in their ultimatum to the head office, and had held their last meeting. The Directors had remained adamant on the question of receiving Erb as spokesman, and the men, not having an orator of equal power in their ranks, and fearful of being worsted in a private interview, had insisted either that Erb should accompany the deputation or that there should be no deputation at all, but only a strike on the following Monday morning. (The advanced party protested against the idea of giving this formal notice of an unlikely event but Erb insisted and the moderates supported him. "If we can get what we want," argued the moderates, "by showing a certain amount of what you may call bluff, by all means let us stop at that.")

It gave Erb a sensation of power to find that not one of these uniformed men in their brass bound caps was strong minded enough or sufficiently clear of intellect to carry out any big scheme by himself; they could only keep of one mind by shoring each other up, and he felt that he himself was the one steady, upright person who prevented them all from slipping. He not only kept them together, but he guided them. A suggestion from him on some minor point of detail, and they followed as a ship obeys the helm; if any began a remark with doubting preface of "Ah, but—" the others hushed them down and begged them to have some sense. Erb had made all his plans for the possible stop of work; the other stations and depots were willing to contribute something infinitesimal every week with much the same spirit that they would have paid to see a wrestling match. All the same, Erb showed more confidence than he felt, and when he left the men, declining their invitation to drink success to the movement (clear to them that Fortune was a goddess only to be appeased and gained over by the pouring out of libations of mild and bitter), he took cheerfulness from his face, and walked, his collar up, along Bermondsey New Road to call for his young sister at her workshop. The sellers on the kerb appealed to him in vain, a shrill voiced little girl thrust groundsel in his face, and he took no notice. Gay bunches of flowers were flourished in front of his eyes, and he waved them aside. If the men went weak at the knees at the last moment it would be deplorable, but it would be an incident for which he could not blame himself; if he himself were to make some blunder in the conduct of the negotiations it would be fatal to his career, and all other secretaries of all other organisations would whisper about it complacently.

"Anxious times, my girl," said Erb to Louisa. "Anxious times. We'll have a tram ride down to Greenwich and back, and blow dull care away."

"I've just finished," said Louisa in a whisper. "I'll pop on me hat, Erb, and be with you in 'alf a moment."

"What's become of your voice?"

"Mislaid it somewhere," said his young sister lightly. "Can't think for the life of me where I put it last."

"This work's beginning to affect your chest," said Erb.

"Funny thing," remarked Louisa, with great good temper, halfway up the wooden stairs of the workshop, "but my medical man ordered me carriage exercise. Shan't be two ticks."

When Louisa returned, stabbing her hat in one or two places before gaining what seemed to be a satisfactory hold, she was accompanied by giggling young women who had been sent by the rest as a commission to ascertain whether it was Louisa's own brother or some other girl's brother who had called for her; Louisa's own statement appearing too absurd to have any relationship to truth. Moreover, presuming it were Louisa's young man who had called for her, it was something of a breach of etiquette, as understood by the girls of the workshop, for one young couple to go out alone, the minimum number for such an expedition being four, in which case they talked not so much to their immediate companion as to the other half of the square party, with whom they communicated by shouting. Having ascertained, to their surprise, that Louisa had spoken the exact and literal truth, they saw the brother and sister off from the doorway, warning Louisa to wrap up her neck, and begging Erb to smile and think of something pleasant.

"Never mind their chaff," said Louisa, in her deep whisper. "I'd a jolly sight rather be going out a bit of an excursion with you than I would with—well, you know."

"Wish you hadn't lost your voice," said Erb, with concern. "I don't like the sound of it, at all."

"There's some girls in our place never get it back, and after about four or five years of it—Don't cross over here."

"Why not?"

"He makes my 'ead ache," said Louisa promptly. "I've only been going out with him for a fortnight, and I know all what he's going to say as though I'd read it in a printed book. He talks about the weather first, then about his aunt's rheumatics, then about the day he had at Brighton when he was a kid, then about where he thinks of spendin' his 'oliday next year, then about how much his 'oliday cost him last year—"

A mild gust of wind came and struck Louisa on the mouth; she stopped to cough, holding her hand the while flat on her blouse.

"Keep your mouth shut, youngster," advised Erb kindly, "until you've got used to the fresh air."

Because both brother and sister felt that in sailing down to New Cross Gate on the top of a tram, and then along by a line less straight and decided to Greenwich they were escaping from worry, they enjoyed the evening's trip. Going through Hatcham, Louisa declared that one might be in the country, and thereupon, in her own way, declared that they were in the country, that she and her brother had been left a bit of money, which enabled her to give up work at the factory and wear a fresh set of cuffs and collars every day: this sudden stroke of good fortune also permitted Erb to give up his agitating rigmarole (the phrase was Louisa's own, and Erb accepted it without protest), and they had both settled down somewhere near Epping Forest; Erb, as lord of the manor, with the vicar of the parish church for slave, and Louisa as the generous Lady Bountiful, giving blankets and home made jam to all those willing to subscribe to Conservative principles. They had a stroll up the hill to Greenwich Park, Lady Louisa forced to go slowly on account of some aristocratic paucity of breath, and Sir Herbert, her brother, playing imaginary games of golf with a stick and some pebbles, and going round the links in eighty two. At the Chalet near the Blackheath side of the park they had tea, Louisa's insistence on addressing her brother by a full title astonishing the demure people at other wooden tables, puzzling them greatly, and causing, after departure, acrimonious debate between husbands and wives, some deciding that Erb and Louisa were really superior people and others making reference to escapes from Colney Hatch. Louisa, delighted with the game of fooling people, darted down the hill, with Erb following at a sedate trot; she stopped three parts of the way down, and Erb found her leaning against a tree panting with tears in her eyes. These tears she brushed away, declaring that something had come to her mind that had made her laugh exhaustedly, and the two went on more sedately through the open way at the side of the tall iron gates, happier in each other's company than in the company of anyone else, and showing this in the defiant way with which some people hide real emotions.

"You're a bright companion," said Louisa satirically, as the tram turned with a jerk at the foot of Blackheath Hill. "You 'aven't made me laugh for quite five minutes."

"I've been thinking, White Face."

"My face isn't white," protested his sister, leaning back to get a reflection of herself in a draper's window. "I've got quite a colour. Besides, why don't you give up thinking for a bit? You're always at it. I wonder your brain—or whatever you like to call it—stands the tax you put on it."

"You'd be a rare old nagger," said Erb, hooking the tarpaulin covering carefully and affectionately around his sister, "if ever anybody had the misfortune to marry you. It'd be jor, jor, jor, from morning, noon, till night."

"And if ever you was silly enough to get engaged, Erb. That's Deptford Station down there," said Louisa, as the tram stopped for a moment's rest. "I used to know a boy who's ticket collector now. He got so confused the other day when I come down here to go to a lecture that he forgot to take my ticket." She laughed out of sheer exultation at the terrifying powers of her sex. "Take my advice, Erb, don't you never get married, even if you are asked to. Not even if it was young Lady Frances."

"Young idiot," said Erb. "Think I ever bother my head about such matters? I've got much more important work in life. This business that I've got on now—"

"Our girls are always asking about you," said Louisa musingly. "It's all, 'Is he engaged?' 'Does he walk out with anybody?' 'Is he a woman 'ater?' and all such rot."

Erb looked down at the traffic that was speeding at the side of the leisurely tram and gave himself up for a while to the luxury of feeling that he had been the subject of this discussion. He thought of his young elocution teacher, and wondered whether he had any right to accept this position of a misogynist when he knew so well that it was made by adverse circumstances and the existence of a good looking youth with an unreliable chin and his hair in waves. The driver below whistled aggrievedly at a high load of hops that was coolly occupying the tram lines; the load of hops seemed to be asleep, and the tram driver had to pull up and whistle again. In a side road banners were stretched across with the word "Welcome," signifying thus that a church bazaar was being held, where articles could be bought at quite six times the amount of their real value. A landau, drawn by a pair of conceited greys, came out of the side street, with a few children following and crying, "Ipipooray!" the proud horses snorted indignantly to find that they were checked by a bucolic waggon and a plebeian tram. A young woman with a scarlet parasol in the landau looked out over the door rather anxiously.

"It's her ladyship," cried Louisa, clutching Erb's arm.

"Good shot," agreed Erb.

"If only she'd look up and recognise us," said Louisa. The other people on the tram began to take an interest in the encounter, and Louisa's head already trembled with pride.

"She wouldn't recognise us."

"Go on with you," contradicted his sister.

Louisa was afflicted with a sudden cough of such eccentric timbre that some might have declared it to be forced. People on the pavement looked up at her surprisedly, and Lady Frances just then closing her scarlet parasol, for the use of which, indeed, the evening gave but little reason, also glanced upwards. Erb took off his hat and jerked a bow, and Louisa noticed that the closed scarlet parasol was being waved invitingly. She unhooked the tarpaulin cover at once, and, despite Erb's protestation that they had paid fares to the Elephant, hurried him down the steps. To Louisa's great delight, the tram, with its absorbedly interested passengers, did not move until the two had reached the open landau, and Lady Frances's neatly gloved hand had offered itself in the most friendly way. Louisa declared later that she would have given all that she had in the Post Office Savings Bank to have heard the comments of the passengers.

"This," said Lady Frances pleasantly, "is the long arm of coincidence. Step in both of you, please, and let me take you home to your place."

"If you don't mind excusing us—" began Erb.

("Oh you—you man," said his sister to herself. "I can't call you anything else.")

"Please, please," begged Lady Frances. They stepped in. By a great piece of good luck,' Erb remembered that amongst the recipes and axioms and words of advice on the back page of an evening paper he had a night or two previously read that gentlemen should always ride with their backs to the horses, and he took his seat opposite to Lady Frances: that young woman, with a touch on Louisa's arm, directed the short girl to be seated at her side.

"Bricklayers' Arms Station, Old Kent Road," said Lady Frances. Mr. Danks, in livery, and his hair prematurely whitened, had jumped down to close the door. Mr. Danks touched his hat, and, without emotion, resumed his seat at the side of the coachman. "You are keeping well, I hope?" To Louisa.

"I have been feeling a bit chippy," said Erb's sister, trying to loll back in the seat, but fearful of losing her foothold.

"So sorry," said Lady Frances. "And you?"

"Thank you," said Erb, "middlin'. Can't say more than that. Been somewhat occupied of late with various matters."

"I know, I know," she remarked briskly. "It is that that makes it providential I should have met you. My uncle is a director on one of the railways, and he was talking about you only last night at dinner."

"Very kind of the gentleman. What name, may I ask?" Lady Frances gave the information, gave also an address, and Erb nodded. "Me and him are somewhat in opposite camps at the present time."

"My uncle was anxious to meet you," said young Lady Frances, in her agreeable way.

"Just at this moment I scarcely think—"

"Under a flag of truce," she suggested. "I was going to write to you, but this will save me from troubling you with a note."

"No trouble."

"I've been opening a bazaar down here," went on Lady Frances with a determined air of vivacity. "The oddest thing. Do you ever go to bazaars?"

"Can't say," said Erb cautiously, "that I make a practice of frequenting them."

"Then let me tell you about this. When you open a bazaar you have first to fill your purse with gold, empty it, and then—"

Louisa sat, bolt upright, her feet just touching the floor of the carriage, and feeling, as she afterwards intimated, disinclined to call the Prince of Wales her brother. Her ears listened to Lady Frances's conversation, and she made incoherent replies when an opinion was demanded, but her eyes were alert on one side of the carriage or the other, sparkling with anxiety to encounter someone whom she knew. Nearly everybody turned to look at them, but it was not until they reached the Dun Cow at the corner of Rotherhithe New Road (the hour being now eight o'clock), at a moment when Louisa had begun to tell herself regretfully no one would believe her account of this gratifying and epoch making event, that into

Old Kent Road, chasing each other, came two girls belonging to her factory. The foremost dodged behind a piano organ that made a fruitless effort to make its insistent jangle heard above the roar and the murmur of traffic; seeing her pursuer stand transfixed, with a cheerful scream of vengeance half finished, she turned her head. At the sight of Louisa bowing with a genteel air of half recognition the first girl staggered back and sat down helplessly on the handles of the piano organ, jerking that instrument of music and causing the Italian lady with open bodice to remonstrate in the true accents of Clerkenwell. When near to Bricklayers' Arms Station Louisa saw again her current young man morbid with the thought of a wasted evening, but still waiting hopefully for his fiancée, now three hours behind time; the young gentleman's eyesight being dimmed with resentfulness, it became necessary for her to wave a handkerchief that might, she knew, have been cleaner, and thus engage his attention. At the very last possible moment he signalled astonished acknowledgment.

For Erb, on the other hand, the journey had something less of exultation. From the moment of starting from St. James's Road, Hatcham, the fear possessed him that he might be seen by some member of his society, who would thereupon communicate facts to colleagues. Thus would his character for independence find itself bruised: thus would the jealousy of the men be aroused; thus would the Spanswick party be able to whisper round the damaging report that Erb had been nobbled by the capitalists. Wherefore Erb, anxious for none of these eventualities, tipped his hat well over his forehead, and, leaning forward, with his face down, listened to Lady Frances's conversation. The carriage had a scent of refinement; the young woman opposite in her perfect costume was something to be worshipped respectfully, and he scarce wondered when, at one point of the journey up the straight Old Kent Road, he heard one loafer say to another, "Where's there an election on to day?" Lady Frances, having completed her account of the bazaar, had information of great importance to communicate, and this she gave in a confidential undertone that was pleasant and flattering.

"From what my uncle says, it appears there is a strike threatening, and—you know all about it perhaps?"

"Heard rumours," said Erb guardedly.

"He is anxious that you should call upon him at the earliest possible moment to discuss the affair privately, but he is most anxious that it should not appear that he has sought the meeting. You quite see, don't you? It's a question of amour propre."

"Ho!" said Erb darkly.

"And I should be so glad," she went on, with the excitement of a young diplomatist, "if I could bring you two together. It would be doing so much good."

"To him?"

"I could drive you on now," she suggested hesitatingly, "and we should catch my uncle just after his dinner; an excellent time."

"I think," said Erb stolidly, "that we'd better let events work out their natural course."

"You're wrong, quite wrong, believe me. Events left alone work out very clumsily at times." Lady Frances touched him lightly on the knee. "Please do me this very small favour."

"Since you put it like that then, I don't mind going up to see him to night. Not that anything will come from it, mind you. Don't let's delude ourselves into thinking that."

"This," cried Lady Frances, clapping her hands, "is excellent. This is just what I like to be doing." Erb, still watching fearfully for acquaintances, glanced at her excited young face, with respectful admiration. "Now, I shall drive you straight on—"

"If you don't mind," said Erb, "no; we'll hop out at the corner of Page's Walk."

"And not drive up to the dwellings?" asked Louisa disappointed.

"And not drive up to the dwellings," said Erb firmly. "I'll get on somehow to see your uncle to night."

"You won't break your word?"

"I should break a lot of other things before I did that."

Thus it was. Lady Frances shook hands; Erb stepped out, looking narrowly through the open gateway of the goods station, and offering assistance to Louisa absently. As he did so, he saw William Henry, his old van boy, marching out of the gates in a violently new suit of corduroys, and with the responsible air of one controlling all the railways in the world.

"Get better soon," said Lady Frances to Louisa. "Mr. Barnes, to night." Mr. Danks, down from his seat and closing the door (Erb and his sister standing on the pavement, Erb wondering whether he ought to give the footman threepence for himself, and Louisa coming down slowly from heaven to earth), Mr. Danks received the order, "Home, please."

Erb went half an hour later by tram to Westminster Bridge and walked across. He perceived the necessity for extreme caution; reading and natural wisdom told him that many important schemes had been ruined by the interference of woman. He looked at the lights that starred the borders of the wide river, saw the Terrace where a member of Parliament walked up and down, following the red glow of a cigar, and he knew that if he were ever to get there it would only be by leaping successfully over many obstacles similar to the one which at present confronted him; to allow himself to be distracted from the straight road of progress would be to court disaster.

"Boy," said the porter at the Mansions, "show No. 124A." In a lift that darted to the skies Erb was conveyed and ordered to wait in a corridor whilst Boy, who wore as many buttons as could be crowded on his tight jacket, went and hunted for Lady Frances's uncle and presently ran him to earth in the smoking room, bringing him out triumphantly to the corridor. Erb found himself greeted with considerable heartiness, invited to come into the smoking room that looked down at a height suggesting vertigo at St. James's Park, taken to a corner, and furnished with a big cigar. Men in evening dress, with the self confidence that comes after an adequate meal, were telling each other what they would do were they Prime Minister, and Erb was surprised to hear the drastic measures proposed for stamping out opposition; some of these seemed to be scarcely within the limits of reason. And what had Erb to say? A plain man, said Lady Frances's uncle of himself (which, in one respect at any rate, was a statement bearing the indelible stamp of truth), always of opinion that it was well to plunge in medias res. On Erb replying that at present he had no remark to offer, the purple faced Director seemed taken aback, and diverted the conversation for a time to Trichinopolies and how best to keep them, a subject on which Erb was unable to speak with any pretence of authority.

"A little whiskey?" suggested the Director, with his thumb on the electric bell, "just to keep one alive."

Lady Frances's uncle sighed on receiving Erb's reply, and proceeded to relate a long and not very interesting anecdote concerning an attempt that had once been made to swindle him by an hotel proprietor at Cairo, and the courageous way in which he had resisted the overcharge. On Erb looking at his silver watch, the colour of the Director's face, from sheer anxiety deepened, and he waved into the discussion with a "Pall Mall Gazette" a silent friend who had been sitting in a low easy chair, with hands clasped over his capacious dress waistcoat, gazing at the room with the fixed stare of repletion. The silent friend craned himself into an upright position and lumbered across the room to the window. The Director, thus usefully reinforced, proceeded to open the affair of the impending strike, and, having done this, urged that there never was a difficulty yet that had not a way out, and demanded that Erb should show this way out instantly. Erb suggested that the Director's colleagues should receive him and the men, listen to their arguments, and concede their requests, or some of them. Director, appealing for the support of the silent man, but receiving none, replied explosively, "That be hanged for a tale!" On which Erb remarked that he had some distance to go, and if the Director would excuse him—Director said, fervently, "For goodness gracious' sake, let us sit down, and let us thresh this matter out." Giving up now his original idea of an exit, he remarked that a golden bridge must be built. Why should not Erb simply stand aside, and let the men alone seek consultation with the Directors? Erb declared that he would do this like one o'clock (intimating thus prompt and definite action), providing there was good likelihood of the men's requests being complied with. Director, looking at silent friend, and trying to catch that gentleman's lack lustre eye, inquired how on earth he could pledge his colleagues. Erb, now interested in the game, suggested that Lady Frances's uncle probably had some idea of the feelings entertained by his fellow directors, and the host, giving up all efforts to get help from his silent friend, admitted that there was something in this. Pressed by Erb to speak as man to man, Director gave the limits of concession that had been decided upon—limits which would not, however, come within sight unless the men came alone, and quite alone, to plead their cause. Erb thought for a few moments, the glare of the silent friend now directed upon him, and then said that he would take Director's word as the word of a gentleman; the men should send a deputation the following day in their luncheon hour, and he (Erb) would stand aside to watch the result. Director offered a hand, and Erb, instinctively rubbing his palm on his trousers, took it, and the silent friend thereupon suddenly burst into speech (which was the last thing of which one would have thought him capable) saying huskily, and with pompous modesty, that he was very pleased to think that any poor efforts of his should have brought about such a happy agreement; that it was not the first time, and probably would not be the last, that he had presided over a meeting of reconciliation, and that his methods were always—if he might say so—tact, impartiality, and a desire to hear both sides.

"Quite glad to have met you," said the Director, also gratified in having accomplished something that would give him the halo of notoriety at to morrow's Board meeting. "You'll go far. Your head is screwed on the right way, my man. Not a liqueur?"

"I take partic'lar care it ain't screwed in any other fashion," said Erb.

"Good bye," said the Director.

"Be good," said Erb.

CHAPTER VII

Erb admitted, at an elocution lesson in Camberwell, that the settlement of the Willow Walk affair had given him a good jerk forward. There was always now a quarter of an hour between the close of his time and the appearance of the next pupil—a quarter of an hour generally occupied by a soliloquy from Erb, prefaced by the cue from Rosalind. "Well now, tell me what you've been doing this week." She had some of the important security that comes to an engaged young woman, and Erb, who looked forward to this weekly exchange of confidences, forced himself to ask politely after Mr. Lawrence Railton, of the "Sin's Reward" Company, and when Rosalind answered (as she usually did) with a sigh that Mr. Railton had not written for some time, Erb made excuses for him on various grounds, such as that he was probably over occupied with the work of his profession, that a man in Mr. Railton's place had to be here, there and everywhere, that it being sometimes the gentleman's affectionate habit to scribble a hurried postcard to his fiancée on the Sunday journeys, likely enough there would be a letter next Monday. On this Rosalind would brighten very much, and sing cheerful words of praise of Mr. Railton, who occupied, it seemed, a unique and delicate position, in that he was much too good for the provinces and not quite good enough for town; nevertheless, "Sin's Reward" had booked a week for the Surrey, and the young woman's bright eyes danced at the thought of seeing him again. Mr. Railton's real name was Botts, which was held to be unattractive as a name on the bills; his father was a silver chaser in Clerkenwell, and it was generally understood that Mr. Railton had had to cut off his parents with a shilling on the grounds that they insisted on calling him Sammy.

Walking home after this fifteen minutes of happiness, Erb found himself continuing the talk, and affecting that Rosalind was tripping along at his side: it was in these silent talks that he dared to call her "dear," thereupon colouring so much that passers by glanced at him curiously; plain faced ladies went on gay with the thought that their features had the power to confuse a stranger. When, in these circumstances, he encountered men of the society they were sometimes greatly diverted, and cried, "'Ullo, Erb. Going over a speech, eh, Erb?"

No doubt at this period of Erb's popularity. His unselfish reticence in the Willow Walk affair, the commonsense he exhibited in one or two minor troubles, the increased polish of the spoken word: all these things increased the men's respect. Also they knew that he worked for them day and night: he had not developed the swollen head of importance that in secretaries of other societies was nearly always a prominent feature. He organised a system of benefits on three scales, by which, if you paid in twopence a week, you received fifteen shillings a week in the case of unjust dismissal; twelve shillings a week for unjust suspension; and ten shillings a week for strike pay. He arranged with a pushful solicitor in Camberwell to give legal advice. He had written one or two articles concerning the society in weekly penny papers, and in these he had taken care not to obtrude his own name or his own work. Even Spanswick admitted now that Erb was turning out better than he had expected, but Spanswick's views might have been brightened by the fact that Erb was organising a ticket benefit at the Surrey on Spanswick's behalf: this not so much on account of any personal misfortune, but because Mrs. Spanswick, always a thoughtless, inconsiderate woman, had mistakenly chosen a time when Spanswick was temporarily suspended from duty for insobriety, to present him with twin babies. "Three," grumbled Spanswick, "three, I could have understood. There'd been a bit of money about three. But two—" Spanswick's friends had promised to rally round him, a feat they performed in theory only, and Erb had to go elsewhere to find buyers of the tickets. Lady Frances had taken a box—a fact which modified and chastened Spanswick's very extreme views in regard to what he usually called the slave owning upper classes. Lady Frances had done a kinder thing than this. On one of her visits to Bermondsey she had met Louisa, white faced and twitching as a result of her work, had gone to Louisa's employer, and had made him shake in his very shoes by denouncing him and all his works, had demanded for Louisa a fortnight's holiday, which the employer, anxious enough to conciliate this emphatic young titled person, and fearful of being sent to the Tower, at once conceded; sent Louisa, with sister Alice for company, away to the country house at Penshurst where the better side of Alice's nature detached itself, and she became an attentive nurse. Erb's Aunt Emma lived at Penshurst: the old lady went up high in the estimation of the other villagers by reason of her nieces' visit to the Court.

The month being July, work well in demand and overtime to be had without asking, Erb was able to obtain consent to almost any project that he liked to submit to his committee. The society was new enough to feel the enthusiasm of youth; the men were pleased with the sensation of power that it gave to them, and they assumed there were no limits to its possibilities. From which causes Erb had several irons heating in the fire, of which one was a new paper to be called "The Carman," to be issued twice a month, and to cost one halfpenny per copy. The expense of production would be something more than this, but when Erb, who was to be managing editor, used that blessed word "propaganda," there was nothing more to be said, and the last doubter gave in.

It was at this time that Erb gave up whistling in the streets.

The white haired labour member had taken him to the House on two occasions, and in the smoking room had introduced him to some wealthy members of the party; and, whilst the board at the side showed the names of unattractive speakers, the members chatted so agreeably that Erb forgot himself occasionally and addressed one who was in evening dress, and had so much money that he wore several coins on his watch chain, as "Sir;" lifting of eyebrows on the part of the labour member told him he had blundered. Members asked questions of Erb, questions which betrayed the fact that their knowledge of the real feelings of the working men was superficial, and thenceforth Erb felt more at his ease. They gave their names as patrons of the Spanswick benefit, and the member who wore coins offered Erb a cigarette, and, seeing him through the outer lobby, begged him to drop a line should anything important occur; this in a way that suggested later to Erb, as he crossed Westminster, that the coin member wanted to find opportunity of becoming attached to some creditable grievance, not so much for the sake of the grievance as for the sake of himself.

"Now," said Erb definitely to the fringe of lights near St. Thomas's Hospital, "I'm not going to be made a cat's paw, mind you."

Interest came with the arrangements for Spanswick's benefit. This necessitated calls at the theatre near the Obelisk in the evenings, and speech with excited men who went about behind the scenes with their hats at the backs of their heads: men who were for ever mislaying letters and documents, and complaining of everybody else's carelessness, and eventually finding the letters or documents in their own hands; the while on the stage some lady in black, with her face whitened, was bewailing to a keenly interested house the perfidy of man, and assuring the gallery of her determination to track down one particular individual, though he should have made his way to the uttermost ends of the earth. The Spanswick night was to be a ticket benefit (which, being interpreted, meant that only the tickets sold outside the theatre would add to Spanswick's income and assuage his present distress), and the night selected was a Friday in the week booked by the "Sin's Reward" Company—Friday, because that was near to the men's pay day, and would hook them at the fleeting moment when spare cash was on the very point of burning a hole in their pockets. Because Lawrence Railton was of the company, and because Erb was responsible for the success of the evening, Rosalind communicated to the scheme the keen interest that became her so well; her father, with ponderous generosity, had promised to ensure a triumphant evening by giving what he termed the considerable advantage of a somewhat long and not altogether undistinguished experience. Erb was anxious to see Lawrence Railton, desirous of seeing what manner of youth had succeeded where he had desired to do so. Matters being as they were, there was no alternative but to play the friend of the family, to meet Mr. Railton with the outstretched hand of amity, to congratulate him, and to save up presently for a wedding present which should represent nicely a genial interest in the welfare of the young couple. A plated cruet stand he thought, as at present advised, but there were arguments in favour of an inkstand that looked like a lawn tennis set— an inkstand had a suggestion of literary tastes that appealed to the prospective editor of "The Carman;" it suggested also a compliment to Rosalind that a cruet stand with the best intentions could never convey. He did not quite know how he would endure it all. Perhaps it would best be remedied by increased application to the work of the society, and if ever the day should come when he found himself elected to a seat in that House at Westminster (the outside of which he went to see very often, just for self encouragement), Rosalind would feel that she might have done better than marry Mr. Lawrence Railton.

"But I don't quite see," admitted Erb, as he wrestled with all this, "I don't quite see what sort of help I shall get out of that."

CHAPTER VIII

At the Obelisk streets radiate, and the trams going to London have to make their choice. The theatre in the road that leads to Blackfriars Bridge is a theatre of middle age, with its own opinion of the many juvenile competitors that have sprung up during recent years in near and in distant suburbs: it endeavours to preserve the semblance of youth and modernity by putting on four white globes of electric light, but its age is betrayed by a dozen women with aprons full of oranges, "Two a punny, a punny for two" (oranges are not eaten in the new theatres), and a tray on high trestles loaded with pigs' trotters, which no one ever buys. Some steps go up to the shilling and the sixpenny seats; early doors, which exact from the over anxious an additional threepence, are in a dark alley at the side, at the end of which is a door that leads to the box office by day and the stage entrance by night. The outside of the house has coloured posters of grisly scenes that make the passer by chill with fear: a yellow woman hurled down a blue precipice; the same lady bound by cords to a grandfather's clock, which shows the hour as three minutes to twelve, and facing her two crape masked men with pistols; underneath the horrid words, "At midnight, my lady, you die." A pleasanter note in the frames of photographs that hang slightly askew. Here, Mr. Lawrence Railton as a wicked Italian (at any rate, his moustache turns upwards, as Gratiano in a third hand costume of the Louis the Fifteenth period, as Inspector Beagle in "Tracking the Criminal," and in as many more characters as the frame will carry). In the centre, Mr. Lawrence Railton as the art of the photographer would have him be in real life, evening dress, insufficient chin, contemptuous smile—the portrait which occupied the position of honour on Rosalind's mantelpiece.

A conspicuous evening for Erb, by reason of the circumstance that he had the honour of conveying Rosalind to the theatre; this because her father, having borrowed individual shillings on individual days from her on the promise of accompanying her had, at the last moment, come into a windfall of two and threepence, and had thereupon remembered an urgent appointment with a dramatist of note at a public house just off the Strand. "Should the fates be kind," said Rosalind's father, "I shall endeavour to honour the performance with my presence later on." Louisa, interested in everything that interested Erb, had organised a raffle at her factory for a circle ticket, and a chapel going girl, who had picked the highest number out of a straw hat accompanied her, with the full anticipation—this being her first visit to the play—that she was about to witness scenes that might well imperil her future existence; unwilling, all the same, to give her prize away or to sell. Erb, confronted with the responsibility of transporting three ladies, had vague ideas of a four wheeler, but remembered in time that this would excite criticism from members ever anxious to detect and crush any effort he might make to commit the unpardonable sin of "putting on side;" compensation came in being allowed to walk by the side of Rosalind, who, near Camberwell Gate, seemed to be dressed prettily but with restraint, but who, as they approached the Elephant and Castle, increased in smartness by contrast with the surroundings of Walworth Road. There were crossings to be managed, and Erb, in the most artful way, assisted her here by insinuating his arm underneath her cape, wondering at his own courage, and rather astonished to find that he was not reproved. Rosalind's manner differed from that of other young women of the district in that she dispensed with the defiant attitude which they assumed, never to be varied from the first introduction to the last farewell.

"And now the question is," said Louisa's colleague, "ought I to go in or ought I to stay outside?"

"Considering you've got a ticket," replied little Louisa satirically, "it seems a pity to go in. Why not stay outside and 'ave an orange instead?"

"Oh," said the chapel goer recklessly, "now I'm here I may jest as well go on with it. In for a penny in for a pound. If the worst comes to the worst, I can shut me eyes and—Who's that lifting his cap to you?"

"'Ullo," remarked Louisa, "you alive still?"

The lad threw away the end of his cigarette, and, advancing, remarked in a bass voice that he had thought it as well to come up on the off chance of meeting Louisa.

"My present young man," said Louisa, introducing the lad.

"Well," said the chapel young woman resignedly, "this is the beginning of it."

Erb, again assisting, took Rosalind up the broad stone staircase; swing doors permitted them to go into the warm, talkative theatre. A few shouts of recognition were raised from various quarters as Erb went in, and he nodded his head in return, but he looked sternly at the direction whence a cry came of "Is that the missus, Erb?" and the chaffing question was not repeated. Down near the stage the orchestra made discordant sounds, the cornet blew a few notes of a frivolous air for practice. Erb bought a programme for Rosalind, and asked if anything else was required; but Rosalind, from a satin bag which hung from her wrist, produced a pair of early Victorian opera glasses, bearing an inscription addressed to her mother, "From a few Gallery Boys," and said, "No, thank you," with a smile that made his head spin round.

"But would you mind," she flushed as she leaned forward to whisper this, "would you mind telling Mr. Railton that I—I should very much like to see him after the show?"

At the stage door a postman had just called, and Erb, waiting for permission to go in whilst the door keeper sorted the letters, could not help noticing that a violet envelope, in a feminine handwriting, was placed under the clip marked R; it was addressed to Lawrence Railton, Esquire. The doorkeeper gave permission with a jerk of the head, as though preferring not to compromise himself by speech, and Erb went up through the narrow corridor where the office and the dressing rooms were situated. Cards were pinned on the door of the latter, and one of them bore, in eccentric type, the name of the gentleman for whom Rosalind had given him the message. A lady's head came out cautiously from one of the other rooms and called in a shrill voice, "Mag gie!" A middle aged woman flew from somewhere in reply with a pair of shoes. Below, the orchestra started the overture of an elderly comic opera; a boy, in a cap, came along the corridor shouting, "Beginners, please!"

"She got in everything for the entire week," said a triumphant voice inside the room, "settled for my washing, cashed up for every blessed thing, and I've never paid the old girl a sou from that day to this. Hullo! what's blown this in?"

Two young men in the small room, and each making up in front of a looking glass; before them open tin cases, powder puffs, sticks of grease paint; bits of linen of many colours. On the walls previous occupiers had drawn rough caricatures: here and there someone had stuck an applauding newspaper notice, or a butterfly advertisement. Neither of the young men looked round as Erb came in, but each viewed his reflection in the looking glass.

"Name of Railton?" said Erb, inquiringly.

"That's me," replied one of the two, still gazing into his looking glass.

"My name's Barnes. I'm secretary to the R.C.A.S."

"Any connection with the press?" asked Mr. Railton, fixing a white whisker at the side of his floridly made up face.

"Not at present!"

"Then what the devil do you mean," demanded the other hotly, "by forcing your way into the room of two professional men? What—"

"Yes," said the man at the other glass, taking up a hand mirror to examine the back of his head, "what the deuce next, I wonder? For two pins I'd take him by the scruff of his neck and pitch him downstairs." He glanced at Erb, and added rather hastily to Mr. Railton: "If I were you."

"I shall most certainly complain to the management," went on Mr. Railton. "It isn't the first time."

"I don't know," said his companion, "what they think the profession's made of. Because we allow ourselves to be treated like a flock of sheep they seem to think they can do just what they damn well please."

"I've a precious good mind," said Mr. Railton, vehemently, "to hand in my notice. Would, too, if it wasn't for the sake of the rest of the crowd."

He ceased for a second, whilst he made lines down either side of his mouth, falling back from the mirror to consider the effect.

"Quite finished?" asked Erb, good humouredly. "If so, I should like to tell you, my fiery tempered warriors, that I have only called with a message from Miss Danks—Miss Rosalind Danks."

"That's one of yours, Lorrie!"

"You mean," said Mr. Railton casually, as he toned down a line with the powder puff, "a dot and carry one girl?"

"Miss Danks," said Erb, "is the leastest bit lame." He repeated precisely the message which Rosalind had given him, and Mr. Railton clicked his tongue to intimate impatience. "I'll call in again later on," said Erb, "when you've finished your little bit, and then I can take you round to where she's sitting."

"Now, why in the world," cried Mr. Railton, throwing a hairbrush on the floor violently, "why in the world can't people mind their own business? There's a class of persons going about on this earth, my dear Chippy—"

"I know what you are going to say," remarked the other approvingly.

"And if I had my will I'd hang the whole shoot of them. I would, honestly."

"I quite believe you would," said Chippy.

"And I'd draw and quarter them afterwards."

"And then burn 'em," suggested Chippy.

"And then burn 'em."

"Would you amiable gentlemen like to have the door closed?" asked Erb.

"Put yourself outside first," recommended Mr. Railton.

The stage and its eccentricities attracted Erb as they attract everyone, and, a licensed person for the evening, he went about through the feverish atmosphere, meeting people who appeared ridiculous as they stood at the side of the stage waiting to go on, but who, as he knew, would look more life like than life with the footlights intervening. Pimple faced men, in tweed caps, hidden from the audience, held up unreliable trees; kept a hand on a ladder, which enabled the leading lady to go up and speak to her lover from the casemented upper window of a cottage; ran against each other at every fair opportunity, complaining in hoarse whispers of clumsiness. A boy came holding clusters of shining pewter cans by the handles, and peace was restored amongst the stage hands, but for the folk in evening dress, with unnatural eyes and amazing faces, who stood about ready to go on, there remained the strain of excitement; some of them soliloquised in a corner, whilst others talked in extravagant terms of dispraise concerning the new leading lady, hinting that no doubt she was a very good girl and kind to her mother, but that she could not act, my dear old boy, for nuts, or for toffee, or for apples, or other rewards of a moderate nature. These seemed to be only their private views, for they were discarded when the leading lady came down the ladder, and they then gathered round her and told her that she was playing for all she was worth, that she had managed to extract more from that one scene than her predecessor had obtained from the entire play, and hinting quite plainly that it was a dear and a precious privilege to be playing in the same company with her. Mr. Lawrence Railton brought for the leading lady a wooden chair; a middle aged bird (who was her dresser) hopped forward bringing a woollen shawl, that had started by being white and still showed some traces of its original intention, to place around her shoulders.

"I don't know," said Mr. Railton, stretching his arms, when, having been ousted from attendance by others, he had strolled up towards Erb, "I don't feel much like acting to night!"

"Do you ever?" asked Erb.

"It's wonderful," went on the young man, "simply and absolutely wonderful the different moods that one goes through, and the effect they have on one's performance. I go on giving much the same rendering of a part for several nights on end, and, suddenly, I seem to get a flash of inspiration."

"Better language!" recommended Erb.

"A flash of inspiration," said the white whiskered young man with perfect confidence, and keeping his eye on the stage. "It all comes in a moment as it were. And then, by Jove! one can fairly electrify an audience. One sees the house absolutely rise."

"And go out?" asked Erb.

On the stage the leading man (who was an honest gentleman farmer, showing the gentleman by wearing patent boots, and the farmer by carrying a hunting crop), cried aloud demanding of misfortune whether she had finished her fell conspiracy against him, and this, it appeared, was the cue for Lawrence Railton in his white whiskers and frock coated suit and a brown hand bag to go on with the announcement that he had come to foreclose a mortgage, information which the house, knowing vaguely that it boded no good to the hero, received with groans and hisses. Erb, watching from the side, prepared for an exhibition of superior acting on the part of Mr. Railton, and was somewhat astonished to find that, instead of playing a part that forwarded the action of the piece, he was a mere butt sent on in order to be kicked off, treatment served out to him by an honest labourer, faithful to his master and with considerable humour in his disposition. Any expectations that Railton would take a more serious part in the melodrama were set aside, in a later scene of Act I., when the hero and the faithful young labourer had both enlisted in a crack cavalry regiment, he came on with his brown bag to find them and give information of importance, and was at once, to the great joy of the pit and gallery, again kicked off, whilst the regiment, consisting of eight men and a girl officer, marched round the stage several times to a military air, and, after the girl officer had delivered a few sentences of admirable patriotism, went off to the Royal Albert Docks to take ship for South Africa. Indeed, throughout the piece it was Mr. Railton's privilege to follow the leading man and his low comedy friend, and whether he encountered them on the quay at Cape Town, out on the veldt near Modder River, or at the Rhodes Club at Kimberley, he was ever hailed by the entire theatre with joyous cries of "Kick him, kick him!" advice upon which the low comedy man always acted.

"D'you like your job?" asked Erb at the end of Act II., as he prepared to go round to the front and collect the men of his committee.

"Someone must hold the piece together," said young Railton, wearily making a cigarette. "Take me away, and the entire show falls to pieces. Even you must have noticed that."

"Upon my word," said Erb, looking at him wonderingly, "you are a perfect marvel. I never saw anything like you."

"Thanks, old chap," replied the other gratefully, and shaking his hand. "Meet me after the show and we'll have a drink together. I was afraid at first you were a bit of a bounder. Don't mind me saying so now, do you?"

"Not at all," replied Erb. "You gave me much the same impression."

"That's most extr'ordinary. There's an idea for a curtain raiser in that. Two men beginning by hating each other, and later on—"

"Any message for your young lady?"

"Which?" asked Mr. Railton.

"You know very well who I mean," said Erb with some annoyance.

"Oh," with sudden enlightenment, "you mean the Danks person. Oh, tell her I'm all right."

Erb looked at him rather dangerously, but the young man, secure in the mailed armour of self content, did not observe this. Erb, placing his doubled fists well down into the pockets of his coat, turned and went off.

"By the bye," called Mr. Railton, in his affected voice.

Erb did not trust himself to answer, but went down the narrow stone passage, and drew a deep breath when he reached the doorway and the dimly lighted alley; he had work to do, and this, as always, enabled him to forget his personal grievances. In the saloon bar of a neighbouring public house he found two members of his committee: because they wore their Sunday clothes they smoked cigars, extinguishing them carefully, and placing the ends in their waistcoat pockets; they came out on Erb's orders to take up position at the stage door. The others were in front of the house, and Erb, going in and standing by the swing door of the circle, discovered them one by one and gave them signal to come out, which they did with great importance, stepping on toes of mere ordinary people in a lordly way.

"Did he send any message?" asked Rosalind anxiously.

"Sent his love." Worth saying this to see the quick look of relief and happiness that danced across her face. "Said he was looking forward to seeing you."

"Ah!"

Three minutes later, when the leading man had done something noble that in the proclaimed opinion of the heroine (there, oddly enough, as a nurse) foreshadowed the inevitable Victoria Cross, and Mr.

Railton had come on in a kilt to be kicked off once more, and there remained only the affairs of England, home, and beauty to be arranged in the last act; the curtain went down, and two minutes later still, the orchestra having disappeared in search of refreshment and the audience occupied in cracking nuts and hailing acquaintances with great trouble at distant points, the curtain went up again on a flapping scene, behind which the tweed capped men, it appeared, were setting an elaborate set for Act IV., doing it with some audible argument and no little open condemnation of each other's want of dexterity. Chairs on the stage stood in a semicircle, and marching on from the left came the dozen members of the committee in their suits of black, twirling bowler hats, and glancing nervously across the footlights in response to the ejaculatory shouting of names. Spanswick, wearing a look of pained resignation, received a special shout, but the loudest cheers were reserved for the secretary, and those in front who did not know him soon took up the cry.

"Erberberberb—"

It became certain at once that Payne was not to give an epoch making speech. Confused perhaps by the footlights, uncertain of the attitude of this great crowded theatre, Payne's memory ran its head against a brick wall and stayed there: he made three repetitions of one sentence, and then, having reversed the positions of the tumbler and the decanter, started afresh, the audience encouraging him by cries of "Fetch him out, Towser, fetch him out," as though Mr. Payne were an unwilling dog, but the same brick wall stood in his way, and, concluding weakly with the remark, "Well, you all know what I mean," he called upon Erb, and sat down glancing nervously across to the pit stalls, where was Mrs. Payne, her head shaking desolately, her lips moving with unspoken words of derision.

"I'm going to take five minutes," said Erb, in his distinct and deliberate way. He took out his watch and laid it on the table. "Even if I'm in the middle of a sentence when that time is up, I promise I'll go down like a shot. I suppose you know the story of the man who—"

Good temper smiled and laughed from the front row of the pit stalls and up to the very topmost row of the gallery at Erb's anecdote, and, hoping for another story, they sat forward and listened. He knew that he held them now, knew they would cheer anything he liked to say, providing he said it with enough of emphasis. He went on quickly that this advantage might not be lost, pounding the palm of one hand with the fist of the other, so that the dullest might know by this gesture when a point was intended; spoke of the good feeling that was aroused by the presence of a fellow man's misfortune; mentioned the work of his own society, urged that so long as this feeling of comradeship existed, so long would their condition improve, not perhaps by a leap or a bound, but by steady, cautious, and gradual progression. Up in the circle his young elocution teacher nodded approvingly, flushing with pride at her pupil's careful enunciation, giving a start of pain at a superfluous aspirate that cleaved the air.

"He can talk," admitted a man behind her.

"If I'd had the gift of the gab," said the man's neighbour, "I could have made a fortune."

Erb stepped out near to the footlights and gave his peroration in an impassioned manner that had the useful note of sincerity. Those in the theatre, who were sympathisers, rose and cheered like a hurricane; the rest, not to be left out of a gratifying show of emotion, joined in, and Spanswick, the hero of the evening, as he rose from his chair to say a few words, might have been a leading politician, a general who had rescued his country from difficulties, or an exceptionally popular member of the Royal Family, instead of a railway carman of third rate excellence with a notable wife.

Spanswick said this was the proudest moment of his life. Spanswick would never forget that night: useless for anybody to ask him to do so. If people should come to Spanswick and invite him to erase that evening from his recollection, he would answer definitely and decidedly, "Never!" So long as memory lasted and held its sway, so long would he guarantee to keep that evening in mind, and carry remembrance with him. Thus Spanswick, in a generous way that suggested he was doing a noble and spontaneous act, and one for which the audience should be everlastingly grateful. Payne, as Chairman, rose, and ignoring a suggestion from the gallery that he should dance a hornpipe, led the group off, the members looking shyly across at the audience, and the audience howling indignantly at one of the men who replaced his hat before getting off.

"Were you nervous, Erb?" asked Louisa excitedly. "I was. Nearly fainted, didn't I?"

"Oh, don't talk," whispered her lady companion, enchanted by the commencement of Act Four. "Don't talk, please, when there's such beautiful things going on."

Mr. Railton had nothing to do in the last act, the dramatist having apparently felt that the thin vein of humour which had been struck in the character was by this time exhausted, and Rosalind looked with anxiety at the curtained doorway of the circle, but Mr. Railton did not appear during the last act, and he was not in the vestibule below when the audience poured out into Blackfriars Road. She was very silent on this, and when Erb saw her into a tram she shook hands without a word. Going back to assist Louisa's young man in the task of escorting the two other ladies, he found himself intercepted by Mr. Lawrence Railton—Railton, in an astrachan bordered coat, and well wrapped around the throat, giving altogether the impression that here was some rare and valuable product of nature that had to be specially protected.

"I want you!" said the young man.

"You'll have to want," said Erb brusquely, and going on.

"But it concerns the girl you were speaking of."

"Where can we go?" asked Erb, stopping.

"Come round to the bar at the back of the circle," said Railton, "and you can give me a drink," he added generously.

A few members of the company were near the bar, and Railton, to compensate for the presence of such an ordinary looking companion, began to talk loudly and condescendingly. Never drank till after the show, he explained, some drank during the performance, but none of the best men did so. One could not give a good reading of the part unless one observed the principles of strict abstemiousness. He flattered himself that he was not one likely to make mistakes, and he held his future, as it were, well and securely in both hands. If Erb would promise not to let the matter go any further, he would show him, in the strictest confidence, a letter from a West End manager, that would prove how near one could be to conspicuous success.

"Not that one," he said, opening a violet envelope. "That's from a dear thing at Skipton. Worships the very ground I walk on."

The letter in question fell on the floor. Erb picked it up and, in doing so, could not help noticing that it began: "Sir, unless you forward two and eight by return, the parcel of laundry will be sold without—"

"Here it is," cried Railton. "'Mr. So and so thanks Mr. Lawrence Railton for his note, and regrets that the arrangements for the forthcoming production are complete.'" "Regrets, you see, mark that! A post earlier, and evidently he would have—don't drown it, my dear chap!"

"In regard," said Erb, putting down the water bottle, "to Miss Rosalind Danks."

"I hadn't finished what I was saying."

"Didn't mean you should. Let's drop your personal grievances for a bit. Why didn't you come round and see her before she left?"

"Now that," said Railton, leaning an elbow on the counter, "goes straight to the very crux of the question. That's just where I wanted to carry you. I hate a man who wastes time on preliminaries. My idea always is that if you've got a thing to say, say it!"

"Well then, say it!"

"My position," said Railton, importantly, "is this. I have, as I think I said, the artistic temperament. I am all emotion, all sentiment, all heart! It may be a virtue, it may be a defect; I won't go into that. The point is that little Rosie is the exact opposite. I confess that I thought at one time that we might be well suited to each other, but I see now that I made a mistake. Doesn't often happen, but I did make a mistake there, and the unfortunate part of the business is that I—in a kind of way, don't you know—promised to marry her."

"So I understood. When does the affair come off?"

"My dear old chap," said Railton, with effusive confidence, "the affair is off. But you know what women are, and I find it rather difficult—for, mind you, I am above all things a man of honour—I find it rather difficult to write to her and tell her so. Some men wouldn't hesitate for a moment. Some men have no delicacy. But what I thought was this: Do you want to earn a couple of pounds?"

"Go on!" said Erb, quietly.

"Assuming that you do want to earn a couple of pounds, this is where you come in. You, I gain, have a certain admiration for her. Now, if you can take her off my hands so that I can get out of the engagement with dignity, I am prepared to give you, in writing mind, a promise to pay—"

Mr. Railton went down swiftly on the floor. The other people hurried up.

"You dare strike me!" he cried complainingly, as he rose his handkerchief to his face. "Do it again, that's all."

He went down again with the same unexpectedness as before. Three men stood round Erb, who looked quietly at his own clenched fist; the knuckles had a slight abrasion.

"Want any more?" he asked.

Mr. Railton made one or two efforts from his crumpled position to speak; the three men suggested police, but he waved his hand negatively.

"Do you want any more, you scoundrel you?" repeated Erb.

"No," answered Mr. Lawrence Railton, weakly, from the linoleum, "I don't want any more. I always know my limit."

CHAPTER IX

This being a period of his life when Erb could do nothing wrong, the unpremeditated experiment with fists had a result that seldom attends efforts of the kind. Railton sent to Erb by post the following day an elaborate letter of apology, in which he argued that Erb, by a quite excusable error, had misunderstood what he (Railton) had intended to convey; that he honoured Mr. Barnes for the attitude he had taken up (which, under similar circumstances, would have been his own), that he should of course carry out his engagement with the young lady whose name it was unnecessary to mention, that he should ever retain an agreeable memory of Mr. Barnes (to whose efforts in the cause of labour he begged in passing to offer his best wishes), he trusted very sincerely that their friendship would not be impaired by the unfortunate incident of the preceding night. Thus Mr. Railton, with many an emphasising underline and note of exclamation, and a flourish under the signature, intended to convey the impression that here was a document of value to be preserved for all time. On Erb discovering his elocution teacher—whose lessons he now scarce required, but whose services as instructress in the art of public oratory he continued for the sheer pleasure of listening to her private speech—on Erb discovering her at his next visit with traces of recent tears he insisted on knowing the cause, and was told, first, that father had been borrowing seventeen shillings and sixpence, which she would have to pay back, amount required in order, the Professor had explained to the credulous lender, to enable him to purchase a comedy which had a part that would fit the Professor like a glove ("I can see myself in it," the Professor declared); and on Erb dismissing this incident as too common for tears, Rosalind reluctantly showed him a letter from the admirable Railton, written by that young gentleman at the same time apparently as the communication he had sent to Erb: in this he regretted time had not permitted him to call at Camberwell Gate, the loss was his; but what he particularly wanted to say was that the farce of their engagement need no longer be allowed to run. On neither side, wrote Mr. Railton, had there been any real affection, and he was sure that this formal intimation would be as great a relief to Rosalind as to himself; he trusted she would find another good fiancé, and he was, with all regards, her friend and well wisher, Lawrence Railton. Erb, greatly concerned for Rosalind, told her nothing of the incident of the benefit performance, but tried to comfort her with the suggestion that Railton had probably written without thought.

"I am beginning to see," said Rosalind presently, "I am beginning to see that I have at least one real friend in the world."

"One's ample," replied Erb stolidly.

With the men of the society the occurrence gave to Erb distinct promotion. Something to have a quick mind with figures, something to be ready of speech, something to be always at hand wherever in London a railway carman was in trouble, but better than all these things was it to be able to think of their secretary as one able to put up his fists. Wherever he went, for a time, congratulations were shouted from the hood of parcels carts or the high seat of pair horse goods vans; boys hanging by ropes at the tail boards giving a cheer as they went by. There is nothing quite so dear and precious as the world's applause, and if here and there a man should announce his distaste for it, the world may be quite sure that this is said only to extort an additional and an undue share. At the next committee meeting Erb was requested, with a good deal of importance, by Payne, as chairman, to be good enough to leave the room for ten minutes: on his return it was announced to him that, moved by G. Spanswick, and seconded by H. R. Bates, a resolution had been carried, according to Herbert Barnes, secretary, an increase in salary of twenty pounds per annum. Erb announced this to his young white faced sister, and added to the announcement an order directing her to leave her factory and look after the home in Page's Walk; but Louisa would not hear of this, declaring that a humdrum life would never suit her, that she should mope herself into a state of lunacy if Erb insisted, and that the money could be laid out much more usefully on, first, a pianoforte; second, a new suite of chairs for the sitting room in place of furniture which had been in the Barnes family for two generations; third, in articles of costume for Erb, and—if any sum remained—in something for herself. They argued the point with desperate good humour from either side of the table, until Erb found that she was really in earnest, and then he gave in.

"You always have your own way, Louisa."

"Precious little use having anybody else's," she retorted sharply.

"You've got a knack of deciding questions," complained her brother, good temperedly, "that makes you a little debating society in yourself."

"There's something in connection with your society," went on Louisa, encouraged, "that you might arrange if you'd got any gumption."

"Let us assume, for the sake of argument, that I have."

"It's this. When one of your single chaps gets engaged let him begin paying into a wedding fund. You've got your strike funds and what not, but you ain't got no wedding fund."

"We haven't any wedding fund," corrected Erb.

"Oh, never mind about grammar," said his young sister impetuously, "I'm talking sense. Let them all pay a bob or so a week, and the one that draws a good number gets his ten pound and goes off and gets married like a shot. See what an interest it'd make the girls take in your society. See how it'd make your young carmen sought after. See how fine it'd be for them to start life on their own, instead of having to go on paying so much a week for 'ire to the furniture shops. See how—"

"A reg'lar little orator," said Erb approvingly. "It must run in the blood, I think. Besides, there's an idea in what you say."

"I never speak," said his sister with confidence, "without I say something." She paused for a moment. "I suppose, Erb, that—that with all this money coming in, you'll begin to think about getting—"

He put his knife and fork down and rose from his chair.

The marriage club was only one of the new features that Erb introduced to the society, but it was the one which had a tinge of melancholy, in that it appeared to him that he was almost alone in not having in hand a successful affair of the heart. Lady Frances came frequently to Bermondsey, where she threw herself with great earnestness into the excellent work of providing amusing hours for children—children who had never been taught games, and knew no other sport than that of imperilling their little lives in the street. Erb, being seen with her one evening as she returned from a Board School, there ensued at the next committee meeting considerable badinage of a lumbering type; Payne declared that Erb should join the wedding club in order that the happy pair should be in a position to set up a house in Portman Square together; Spanswick remarked with less of good temper, that some people's heads were getting too big for their hats; whilst other members, ever ready to take part in the fine old London sport of chipping, offered gibes. Erb retorted with his usual readiness, and laughed at the suggestion; but afterwards found himself fearing whether Lady Frances was, in point of fact, lavishing upon him a hopeless affection. He had almost persuaded himself to admit that this was the case, when his sister Alice made one of her condescending calls at Page's Walk and gave, with other information, the fact that the sweetheart of Lady Frances, a lieutenant, the Honourable Somebody, had some time since been ordered away on a mission to the North West Coast of Africa; her young ladyship was, by this desperate interest in the juveniles of Bermondsey, endeavouring to distract her mind from thoughts of her absent lover. Erb breathed again and gave assistance in managing the most trying boys at the "Happy Evenings." One night, as he performed the duty of seeing Lady Frances through the dimly lighted streets to Spa Road Station, they met Rosalind and her father. Rosalind flushed hotly, and Erb wondered why. He demanded of her the reason at the next elocution lesson, and Rosalind said calmly, that it was because at that moment she had given her second best ankle a twist.

Lady Frances brought to Erb an invitation that flattered him. Her uncle, of Queen Anne's Mansions, a man in most of the money making schemes of London, but one never anxious to obtrude his own name or his own personality, felt desirous of starting a movement for (to give the full Christian names) "The Anglicising of Foreign Manufactures."

This Lady Frances explained to him, with her usual vivacity, the while both kept an eye on some noisy Bermondsey infants, who were playing in the hall of the Board School.

"Other countries are getting ahead of us, my uncle says, and unless something is done at once, British trade (Now, children, do play without quarrelling, please, to oblige me!), British trade will go down, and down, and down, and there will be nothing left."

"Are things really so bad?"

"Oh, they're terrible," declared Lady Frances, with great cheerfulness. "Apparently the bed rock has almost been reached, and it is only by a great and a unanimous effort that Great Britain will ever again be enabled to get its head above water. So, at any rate, my uncle tells me."

"I don't know—(Young Tommy Gibbons, if I catch you at that again you know what will happen)—I don't know that I've ever studied the subject in the large. My own society takes up nearly all my time, and other work I leave to other people."

"Exactly, Mr. Barnes, exactly! I quite understand your position. But I have such faith in my uncle. Do you know that nearly everything he touches turns into money."

"Very agreeable gift."

"But the point is this, that nothing can be done unless capital and labour work in unison for a common end. One is affected quite as much as the other, and alone neither can do anything. British trades are being snapped up by America, by France, by Germany, even by Belgium, the only remedy, my uncle says, is for us to take some of their manufactures and plant them here.—(I was sure you'd fall down and hurt your knee, little boy. Come here and let me kiss the place and make it well)—I don't know whether I make myself quite plain to you, Mr. Barnes?"

"In one sense you do," said Erb. "Only thing I can't see is, where your uncle imagines that I come in."

A dispute between two children over a doll necessitated interference, based on the judgment of Solomon.

"Obviously," replied the girl, delighted at the importance of her task, "obviously, your work will be to organise."

"Organise what?"

"Meetings of working men to take up the idea, discussion in the halfpenny papers, argument in workshops. In this way," she said, with her engaging frankness, "in this way, you see, you could strengthen my uncle's hands."

"Not sure that that is the one desire of my life."

"I am so clumsy," deplored Lady Frances.

"Not more than most people."

"If you would only see my uncle and argue it out! He, I am sure, would succeed where I," with a sigh, "where I so horribly fail."

"Look here," said Erb, hastily, "if it's any satisfaction to you, I'll say at once that I'm with the movement, heart, body, and soul."

Lady Frances took his big hand and patted it thankfully.

"Can't tell you how pleased I am," she declared. "I'll send on all the circulars and figures and things when I reach Eaton Square to night—(Children, children, you are tiresome, really)—and then you can start work directly, can't you?"

A busy man always has time to spare; it is only your lazy person who can never place a minute at anyone's disposal. Thus it was that Erb tacked on to his other duties, the work of making known the Society for Anglicising Foreign Manufactures, pressing into the service all the young orators of his acquaintance, and furnishing them with short and easy arguments. Our import trade was so many millions in excess of our outgoing trade: why should this be so? Our villages were becoming deserted, and country manufactories dwindled day by day: this must be stopped. Vague talk about technical education; praise for the English working man, and adulation of his extraordinary, but sometimes dormant brain power; necessity of providing tasks for the rising generation that they might not push men of forty out of berths. An agreeable programme, one that could be promulgated without those submissive inquiries addressed to the labour leaders in the House, which always had a suggestion of servility. Erb, the following Sunday, spoke at Southwark Park in the morning, at Peckham Rye in the afternoon, and Deptford Broadway in the evening, and, the subject being new, he found himself invited to address several working men's clubs during the week. Paragraphs, slipped into the newspapers, sometimes contained his name: Lady Frances wrote that her uncle was delighted, and had asked to be especially remembered. A later note mentioned that it was intended to hold a mass meeting at St. James's Hall, to bring the subject well before the people of London: her uncle would not be able to be present, but he had begged her to request Mr. Barnes to speak on this occasion: there would be a Duchess of philanthropic tendencies in the chair, and several members of Parliament had promised to speak. "Don't disappoint us!" said the postscript appealingly. Erb sent an agreeable postcard in reply, and a friend of his, an assistant librarian in the Free Library, promised to devote himself to work of research and ascertain how one addressed a lady of such distinguished rank as the wife of a Duke. The assistant librarian urged that evening dress was the correct thing, and offered to lend a suit which he and his brother wore when they went out into society, patronising dances at the Surrey Masonic Hall but here Erb's commonsense interfered. The meeting was advertised in the daily papers and on hoardings, his name given as Herbert Barnes, Esquire, with full qualifications set out: he never saw one of the posters without stopping to enjoy the sight, and it pained him extremely to find that on one or two in the neighbourhood of home some friend had erased the affix. Louisa went boldly one evening to the offices of the new society, in College Street, Westminster, and obtained a copy of the poster; this she would have exhibited in the front window, but compromised by sticking it at its four corners on the wall of the sitting room.

St. James's Hall was not over crowded on the evening, and a wealthy member of the committee went about telling everybody that a smaller room would have been cheaper, but it was full enough to please Erb as he took a view of it from the stairs leading to the platform. The platform was fringed with palms; on the walls were hung banners, with quotations from Shakespeare down to the newest poet; quotations, that appeared to give vague support to the movement. Lady Frances, hovering about in the manner of an anxious butterfly, introduced Erb to the Duchess, and the Duchess, without using her lorgnon, said beamingly that she had read all of Mr. Barnes's works, and felt quite too delighted to meet the author; Erb protested nervously that he had never written a book, but the Duchess waved this aside as ineffective badinage, and went on talking the while she looked away through her glasses at arriving people. So delighted, said the Duchess absently, to mingle with men of talent; it took one into another atmosphere. The Duchess, for her part, claimed to have powers of observation, and trusted piously that she was not altogether without a sense of humour, but these exceptional qualities, she said, had never availed her when she took pen in hand. Erb, perceiving the futility of contradiction, suggested that she should one day, when a spare moment arrived, have another dash at it, and the Duchess, bringing her gaze by a process of exhaustion round to him, stared at him wonderingly for a moment, and then promised to act upon his advice. A shy little man of letters being submitted just then to her consideration, the Duchess dropped Erb, and engaged in animated monologue on the subject of labour and how to conciliate it: her own method seemed to be to treat it as an elephant and give it buns. Erb stood about the room, whilst well dressed people flew one to the other with every sign of gratification; he felt all his usual difficulty of not knowing what to do with his hands. The people had a manner of speech that he could understand with difficulty, they talked of things that for him were a sealed book.

Three clergymen who came in a bunch and seemed similarly out of the movement, gave him a feeling of companionship. When they all formed in a line and marched up on the platform to a mild, whispered cheering from the Hall, Erb's interest quickened, and the slight feeling of nervousness came which always affected him when he was going to speak.

"And I do think," said the Duchess, with shrill endeavour to make her voice reach the back of the hall, "I do think that the more we consider such matters the more likely we are to understand them and to realise what they mean, and to gain a better and a wider and a truer knowledge." The three clergymen said, "Good, good," in a burst of respectful approbation, as men suddenly illuminated by a new thought. "I am tempted to go further," said the Duchess, waving her notes threateningly at the audience, "to go further, and express myself, if I may so say, that having put our hands to the plough—" She looked round at the straight line of folk behind her, and they endeavoured to convey by their looks that if a Duchess could not be allowed the use of daring metaphor, then it would have to be denied to everybody. "Having put our hands to the plough, we shall not turn back—(slight cheering)—we shall not falter—(renewed slight cheering)—we shall not loiter by the roadside, but we shall go steadily on, knowing well that—that—" Here the Duchess found her notes and read the last words of her peroration carefully, "knowing well that our goal is none other than the rising sun, which symbolises so happily the renaissance—" Here she looked down at the reporters' table, and seemed about to spell the word, but refraining contented herself by saying it again with great distinctness. "The renaissance of British Trade and British Supremacy!"

A service member of Parliament proposed the first resolution, and did so in a speech that would have suited any and every occasion on sea or land, in that it was made up entirely of platitudes, and included not one argument that could be seized by the most contentious; the whole brightened by what the member of Parliament himself described as a most amusing discussion which he had held with a man of the labouring classes not many years since (on which occasion the member had travelled second, this being notoriously the only way of discovering the true aspirations of the lower classes), and the member had subjected the man to a rigid cross examination of the most preposterous and useless nature which he now repeated with many an "Ah, but I said—" and "Now listen to me, my good fellow—" and "Permit me to explain what I mean in simple words so that even you can understand," the labouring man eventually giving in (so, at any rate, the Member declared), admitting that the gallant Member had won the game at every point—the probability being that the poor fellow, bullied and harried by a talkative bore, had done so in the interests of peace and with a desire to be let alone and allowed to read his evening paper. The service Member clearly prided himself not only on the acuteness which he had displayed in the argument, but also on the wonderful imitative faculty which enabled him to reproduce the dialect of his opponent, a dialect which seemed to have been somewhat mixed, for in one instance he spoke Lancashire with, "Aye, ah niver thowt o' that," and the next broad Somerset, "There be zummat in what yew zay, zir," and anon in a strange blend of Irish and Scotch.

"'That this meeting calls upon the working classes to put aside all differences and to contribute their indispensable assistance to the new movement, from which they themselves have so much to gain.' Will Mr. Herbert Barnes please second?"

This was written on the slip of paper, and passed along to Erb at a moment when the grisly fear had begun to possess him that he might not be called upon at all. He nodded to the secretary, and felt that the audience, now tired of listening to spoken words, looked at him doubtfully. One of the three clergymen being selected to move the resolution, the other two looked at their shoes with a pained interest, and presently tugged at their black watch guards, ascertained the time, and, just before the chosen man arose, slipped quietly out. Fortunately for Erb, the remaining clergyman started on a line of reasoning excellently calculated to annoy and to stimulate. Began by pointing out that everybody nowadays worked excepting the working man, doubted whether it was of much use offering to him help, but declaring himself, in doleful tones, an optimist, congratulated the new movement on its courage, its altruism, its high nobility of purpose, and managed, before sitting down, to intimate very defiantly that unless labour seized this unique opportunity, then labour must be left to shift for itself and could no longer expect any assistance from him.

"Ladies and gentlemen!" said Erb distinctly. The promise of listening to a voice that could be heard without difficulty aroused the Hall. "I should be glad if the gentleman who spoke last could spare just three minutes of his time, and refrain for that space from making a hurried and somewhat undignified departure from the Hall." The clergyman who had adopted the crouching attitude of those who desire to escape furtively from close confinement, returned and sat, his back straightened. "He has spoke—I should say, he has spoken—in a patronising way of labour, and I want to tell him that we resent very strongly his condescending and almost contemptuous words."

His predecessor rose and said, "May it please your—"

"No, no, no!" said Erb, with but a slight modification of his Southwark Park manner, "I didn't interrupt the reverend gentleman, and I'm not going to allow him to interrupt me. Or to assume the duties, your Grace," with a nod to the chair, "which you perform with such conspicuous charm and ability."

The Duchess, who, fearing a row, had been anxiously consulting those around her in order to gain hints as to procedure, recovered confidence on receiving this compliment, and gave a smile of relief. Men at the table below adjusted their black leaves of carbonic paper and began to write.

"Now, I've been into the details almost as carefully as the reverend gentleman has, and what I want to say, in order that this audience should not consider that we are absolutely silly fools, is, that so far from this movement having been arranged in order to benefit the workers exclusively, it is very clear to me that there's a few behind the scenes who are going to make a bit out of it."

One cry of approval came from the distant gallery, but this scarcely counted, for it was a voice that had applauded contrary statements with the same decision. Erb knew the owner of the voice, a queer old crank, who went about to public meetings, his pockets bursting with newspapers, more than content if in the Free Library the next day he should find but one of his solitary cries of "Hear, hear," reported in the daily press.

"I've no doubt they feel pretty certain of a safe eight or ten per cent.; if they didn't, this meeting would never have been held, and we should have been denied the pleasure of listening to that lucid and illuminating speech with which your Grace has favoured us. I say this that the previous speaker may see and that you all may recognise the fact that if those I represent give the cause any assistance, we do so with our eyes wide open, and that we are not blindfolded by the cheap flannel sort of arguments to which we have just listened. But let me go on. Because this is going to be a soft thing for the capitalists, it by no means follows that it is going to be a hard thing for the worker. On the contrary! I can see—or I think I can see—that this is likely to benefit both of us. (Cheers.) And whilst I repudiate the attitude and the arguments of the last speaker, I promise you that I am prepared to do all that I can for the scheme— (cheers)—not in the interests of capital, for capital can look after itself, but in the interests of labour, which sometimes wants a lot of looking after. Your Grace, I beg to second the resolution."

Not a great speech by any means, but one with the golden virtue of brevity, and one spoken with obvious earnestness. The Hall liked it; the subsequent speakers made genial references to it, and the Duchess, in acknowledging a vote of thanks, repaid Erb for his compliment to herself by prophesying that Mr. Barnes would prove a pillar of strength to the cause, declaring graciously that she should watch his career with interest, and gave him a fierce smile that seemed to hint that this in itself was sufficient to ensure success. (Later, when he said goodbye, the Duchess called him Mr. Blenkinsop, and begged him to convey her kindest regards to his dear wife.)

"I wonder," said a gentleman with concave spectacles, "I wonder, now, whether you have a card about you?"

"Going to do a trick?" asked Erb.

"Here's mine. Have you ever thought of entering the House?"

"Someone would have to provide me with a latch key."

"I take you!" remarked the spectacled gentleman adroitly. "Don't happen to be Welsh, I suppose, by any chance? Ah! a pity!"

For a moment it occurred to Erb that this might be a sample of aristocratic chaff; he stopped his retort on seeing that the other was talking with perfect seriousness. "But something else may happen at any moment. We live in strange times."

"We always do," said Erb.

"I shall keep you in my mind."

Lady Frances eluded some dowagers who were bearing down upon her, and came to him; she took an envelope from a pretty hiding place.

"My uncle particularly begged me to give you this. You were so good, Mr. Barnes. (Don't open it until you get home.) Your speech was just what one wanted. You quite cleared the air."

"Afraid I should clear the 'All." Lady Frances seemed not to comprehend, and the knowledge came to Erb that he had missed an aspirate.

"My uncle will be so pleased. I shall be down at Bermondsey next week, and I can bring any message my uncle wishes to send. I don't bother you, Mr. Barnes?"

"Need you ask?" replied Erb.

"You're not going?" with her gloved hand held out.

Erb took the hint and made his exit with difficulty, because several ladies buzzed around him, humming pleasant words. The spectacled man walked with him along Piccadilly, talking busily, and expressed a desire to take Erb into the club for coffee. "Only that my place is so deucedly uncivil to visitors." He contented himself with a threat that Erb should most certainly hear from him again.

"I shan't lose your address," said the spectacled person.

It was not until the Committee Meeting of the R.C.S. had nearly finished one evening that Erb, in searching for a letter which some members desired to see, found the note from Lady Frances's uncle. He tore the flap casually, and, recognising it, placed the opened envelope aside, and pursued his searches for the required document. Spanswick, with a busy air of giving assistance, looked through the letters, and opened the communication which Lady Frances had brought.

"Pardon, old man," whispered Spanswick confidentially. "Didn't know I was interfering with money matters."

CHAPTER X

It is the ingenious habit of Kentish railways directly that hop picking is over and pay day is done, to advertise excursions to London at a fare so cheap that not to take advantage of it were to discourage Providence in its attempts to make the world pleasant. Country folk, who make but one visit a year to town, seize this September opportunity; some avail themselves not only of this but of the Cattle Show trip later on; a few also take the pantomime excursion in February, and these are counted in quiet villages as being, by frequent contact with town, blades of the finest temper, to whom (if they would but be candid) no mysteries of the great town are unknown. Erb's Aunt Emma, giving herself reward for a month's hard work in the hop garden, came up every year by the September excursion. It happened on this occasion that the day could not have made a more awkward attempt to fit in with Erb's convenience.

"Well," said Aunt Emma, in the 'bus, desolately, "I'm not surprised! It's what comes of looking forward to anything. When I heerd as you may say, you'd left the railway, I said to the party that comes in on Mondays to help me do my week's washing, 'I don't know,' I says, 'what to think 'bout all this.'"

"Any other day, almost," urged her nephew, "I could have arranged for the day off, but I've got important work to do that'll take me up to nine o'clock."

"Whenever I find a bit of a lad giving up a honest living, I always say to Mrs. Turley, I say, 'Dang it all, this won't do!' And when it 'appened to my brother's own boy I turned round at once, I did, and I said, 'I don't know what to—'"

"If Louisa had been quite herself, why, of course, she—"

"I'll get back to Lonnon Bridge," said Aunt Emma grimly. "Reckon I shall be some'ing like Mrs. Turley's eldest. He come up one November, he did—first time he'd been to Lonnon—and it were a bit foggy, so he kep' in the station all day; when he come home, he says, 'Mother,' he says, 'it's a fine big place, Lonnon is, but it dedn't quite come up to my expectations.'" The parchment faced old lady was pleased by Erb's reception of this anecdote, and, gratified also to get a smile from other passengers, she relaxed in manner; Erb saw the opportunity.

"Tell you what we've arranged, Aunt Emma. Louisa and me talked it over as soon's ever we made out your letter—"

"I don't perfess," remarked the old lady, "to be first class in me spellin'. 'Sides, I got someone else to write it."

"And we decided that we'd get a friend of mine—a friend of ours to look after you for the day."

"What's he like?" asked the old lady, with reluctant show of interest.

"It's a she!"

"Your young woman?"

"I don't go in for anything of that kind," said Erb, looking round the 'bus apprehensively. "Too busy for such nonsense."

"Never knew the man yet," said Aunt Emma, "that couldn't make time to get fond of somebody."

Arrived at the office at Grange Road, Erb was showing the aunt some of his newspaper notices, when he heard on the stairs the swish of skirts. He lost the remaining half of his remark.

"And you've been fairly walking out, then, as you may say, with our Lady Frances?"

"You can't call it that, Aunt. I've only just been paying her polite attention."

"I know what you mean," remarked the old lady acutely. "Her grandmother—I'm speaking now of forty year ago, mind you—her grandmother ran off with a—let me see! Forget me own name next."

Erb answered the quiet tap at the open door.

"Good girl!" he cried cheerfully. "Welcome to our baronial hall! Aunt Emma, this is the young lady that's going to pilot you round. Almost makes you seem," he said to Rosalind, "like one of the family."

"I only had to put off three pupils," said Rosalind quickly. "How do you do?"

"I'm going downstairs to fetch coffee and scones for you two," announced Erb. "Try not to come to blows whilst I'm away."

"My sciatica is just beginning to wake up, as you may say," replied Aunt Emma.

"So sorry," said Rosalind sympathetically. "It must interfere with getting about."

"Thank you," replied Aunt Emma coldly. "I'm able to set up and take nourishment."

"I expect your nephew has a lot of callers," she said with determination. "He knows a good many people."

"Are you acquainted with our Lady Frances," asked the aunt in a mysterious whisper.

"I have just seen her," flushing a little for some reason.

"These upper classes, they don't stand at nothing, as you may say, when—" Erb returned, and the aunt, with the wink of a diplomatist, raised her voice. "They paid eight to the shillin' this year it ought to've been seven. I said so straight, all through the hopping, I did, to Mrs. Turley."

The doors were to open at two for the afternoon's entertainment, and the aunt's idea was that it were well to get there by noon, and thus ensure the best value in seats for a shilling; Rosalind gently over ruled this, and they went first to Westminster Abbey, at which the aunt sneered, saying it was not her idea of a place of worship, and to the National Gallery, in regard to the contents of which the old lady hinted that they compared badly with a rare set of illuminated almanacks which she had at home, issued yearly by Deane, the grocer; the almanacks, it appeared, had the advantage of giving the date of jolly nigh every month you could think of. Trafalgar Square, looked on as a square, the aunt thought not much better than middling; the Embankment, in her opinion, lacked many of the attractions that she remembered once to have found at Ramsgate. But when, later, they were seated in the front row of the gallery in a small hall, and the curtain went up disclosing a crescent of black faced men, with instrumentalists behind them, and similarly coloured gentlemen, with be frilled shirtfronts, at either end asked riddles of the gentlemanly man at the centre, riddles of which the gentlemanly man almost alone in the Hall knew not the answer, able only to repeat the question in a sonorous manner, then Aunt Emma relinquished all attempt at criticism, and gave herself up to pure delight. "Can you tole me, Mithter Johnthon, how a woman differth from an umbrella?"

"Can I tell you," repeated the gentlemanly man very distinctly, "how a woman differs from an umbrella?"

"Now 'ark for the answer!" whispered Aunt Emma, nudging her young companion gleefully.

"No, sir," said the gentlemanly man, "I cannot tell you how a woman differs from an umbrella."

"You can't tole me how a woman differth from an umbrella? Why," explained the corner man, "you can shut an umbrella up!"

"How in the world they think of all these things!" said Aunt Emma exhaustedly. "Dang my old eyes if it 'ent a miracle!"

Aunt Emma wept when a thin voiced youth sang, "Don't neglect your mother 'cause her hair is getting grey," became hysterical with amusement over, "I'm a gay old bachelor widow." Rosalind found herself enjoying the enjoyment of the old lady, and when they came out into daylight, and went across the way to a noble establishment, where they had high tea, the two were on excellent terms with each other, and information regarding small scandals of Penshurst was placed freely at Rosalind's disposal. The old lady spoke in an awed whisper when she came to the people at the Court, and arrested a slice of ham on her fork, as though sensible of the demands of etiquette when dealing with the upper classes.

"You're not married, my dear," said Aunt Emma, loosening the strings of her bonnet and allowing it to fall to the back of her head in an elegant way, "or else I could speak more free, as you may say, on the subject. That grandmother of hers—" The old lady pursed her lips, and glanced at her reflection in the mirrored walls with a pained shake of the head.

"But," urged Rosalind, perturbed by the aunt's confident manner of prophecy, "Lady Frances, I understand, is engaged to a lieutenant out in North Africa."

"Then sooner he comes back," shaking a spoon threateningly, "sooner he comes back the better. I don't want to go opening my old mouth too wide, or else like enough I shall go and put my foot in it. I've said all I want to say, and I don't want folk to turn round arterwards and say to me, 'Why didn't you give us warnin'?' Strikes me, my dear, we might have drop more hot water with this yere tea."

"Do you know her uncle at all?"

"I know of him. I used to be upper housemaid at the Court."

"And what—"

"I don't think no worse of him," said Aunt Emma in a slow, careful, and judicial manner, "I don't think no worse of him than what he's thought worse of."

"I see," said Rosalind doubtfully. The girl was silent for a few moments. She looked at the walnut face of Erb's aunt, at the elderly dimple beside the mouth, she watched the old lady's cautious way of munching food.

"What you thinking of, my dear?"

"Nothing, nothing," said Rosalind, arousing herself.

"You won't 'spect me to finish up these yere bits I hope," said Aunt Emma, looking at the crusts by the side of her plate. "My teeth ain't what they was when I was your age. Ah," with a sigh, "that seems long time ago."

"You have never been married, have you?"

"Could ha' been," said the old lady shortly. "'Twarnt for want of being asked."

"Why, of course not."

"Only chap I ever wanted," she said reminiscently, "I let him go and get snapped up by someone else; silly bit of a gel that I was. I tell ye what 'tis!"

People at the neighbouring tables were listening, and Rosalind touched her wrinkled hand gently to call her attention to the fact.

"Once you've made up your mind, as you may say, about a young man, you've got to be jeggerin' well careful you don't go and lose him. Makes all the difference whether you get the right man or the wrong man, or no man at all. Now what about this Drury Lane? We'd bedder be too soon than too late."

A wonderful old person for her age, and Rosalind, made rather thoughtful for some reason by the conversation, had much ado to keep up with her as they walked through Leicester Square and Long Acre in the direction of Autumn Melodrama. When the doors opened, Erb's aunt fought her way in with the best of them, securing two seats in the second row, and keeping strong men and insurgent women at bay until Rosalind came up; she ordered a very tall man in the front row to sit down, and when he replied that he was a sitting down Aunt Emma suggested that he should lie down. Then the old lady loosened her elastic sided boots slightly, and prepared to meet enjoyment.

A great evening. Aunt Emma confessed to Rosalind, as they came out, that, say what you liked, there was no place like London, and, but for the fact that she wanted to save the bit of money she had put away, she would willingly bid good bye to Penshurst and come up to town, spending every afternoon at Moore and Burgess', and every evening at Drury Lane. Outside the theatre was Erb.

"Nice young woman, if ever there was one," whispered Emma to her nephew. "Superior manner, and all that."

"Thought you'd get along all right with her," remarked Erb.

"I've been giving her advice."

"Trust you."

"Wonnerful to see such qualities of people about," said the old lady, hailing Rosalind into the discussion as they walked along the crowded Strand. "Nothin like this down where I live."

"Have you far to walk at the other end?" asked the girl solicitously.

"Not fur," replied the wonderful old lady. "Ony 'bout four mile and h'af."

The excursion train was nearly ready to start, and Erb, finding an old acquaintance in the guard, arranged for appropriate finish to a great day by placing his aunt in a first class compartment. She remarked gleefully that this would be something to tell Mrs. Turley.

"God bless ye, my dear," she said, kissing Rosalind. "And don't forget what I told you. Erb, take care of her."

Rosalind wanted to go into the Strand telegraph office opposite the station for a moment, if Erb did not mind. Erb did not mind, and he waited.

"As much as that?" said Rosalind to the clerk. "Seems a lot of money."

"Well, you see, miss," replied the clerk, apologetically, "people don't telegraph to these distant parts unless it's about something important."

CHAPTER XI

"My dear Mr. Barnes," wrote Lady Frances' uncle in a genial note, dated from a Pall Mall club, "I am sorry my niece did not make my intention more apparent; possibly the mistake was my own. I never dreamt of offering you, as you assume, anything in the shape of a bribe. What I thought was that, as one who had the interests both of capital and labour at heart, I might be allowed to make a small contribution towards any movement in which you were interested. You mentioned once an idea of starting a small paper; let my small cheque assist in this excellent effort.

"I was glad to see your admirable speech so fully reported in the newspapers. The new movement owes much to your influential voice. I think we shall want you to run down to Birmingham next week, but the secretary will write you, and he also will see to the expenses. If you will not accept payment for your services, at any rate there is no reason why you should be out of pocket over the business.—Yours with great regard."

"Reads fair enough," commented Erb. "I may have worded my letter a bit too harsh."

From Birmingham the party went to Stafford and to Coventry, all somewhat in the manner of a travelling theatrical company, the party including, indeed, some eccentrics which emphasised the resemblance. There was an Irish barrister, who had hitherto pleaded mainly at Cogers' Hall, and had a change in temperament for every glass of whiskey that he drank, going up and up the hill of cheerfulness until a certain number was reached, whereupon each succeeding glass made him descend slowly to the tableland of contempt for the world; a young Oxford man eager to make some alteration in the world without delay; and one or two safe men, who could always be relied upon to say a few appropriate words. Erb sent to Rosalind from each town press notices, with crosses near to the references to himself, until it suddenly occurred to him that these signs might have two meanings; afterwards he drew a rather clumsy hand to draw attention to the only item in the papers worthy of Rosalind's notice.

Erb was now so much in the movement of life that he experienced a kind of restless fever unless he had some new project in hand. He felt ashamed to confess himself hurt on his journey back to town when he found names of other labour leaders endowed with the importance of print, and a newspaper which did not contain his name appeared to him to have been scarce worth the trouble of setting up; this was emphasised by the fact that the Irish barrister, on seeing him off, had given him a generous compliment; patting him on the back, he had assured Erb that the name of Barnes was one that would be engraven in imperishable letters of gold on the temple of Fame, and that he, for his part, would never, never forget him. Small wonder, with this feeling of self importance, that Erb should give but little attention to the fact that Louisa was at home in Page's Walk, looking paler than usual. Louisa remarked that she was really only playing truant, having made up her mind not to work so hard in future. "They think all the more of you," said Louisa acutely.

A storm seldom occurs without some premonitory signs, and it was on the tramcar that took him to Camberwell—no reason why he should go to Camberwell other than his desire to see Rosalind, and this would make him late for the committee meeting—it was on the tramcar that the first warnings appeared. Erb was seated at the back reading the manuscript, an article commencing, "Brother Workers!" when two men in railway uniform came up the steps, so keenly engaged in conversation that they stopped half way to settle some disputed point, barring the descent of passengers who wished to alight. When, at the strenuously worded request of the delayed passengers, and the mild appeal of a tame conductor, they were induced to move, they scampered up, and taking seats immediately in front of Erb, recommenced their argument. One was a member of Erb's society; the other, a man who had obstinately kept outside. Erb would have spoken to them, but that he was just then in a state of ecstatic admiration over what seemed to him a well turned sentence in the article.

"Tell you what it is, old man," said the non member, slapping his corduroyed knee emphatically. "You've been makin' a little tin god of the chap, and, naturally enough, he's taken advantage of it. You pass him votes of thanks, and what not, and fill him up with soft soap, and consequence is, he goes swelling about, and—"

"He wasn't far wrong about that South Western business," remarked the other with meek determination, "and chance it."

"You can't expect a man not to do right sometimes. I ain't arguin', mind you, that Erb's a fool. Far from it! My view of the matter is, if you must know—"

"I never ast for your opinion!"

"Never mind whether you ast for it or not. My view of the whole matter is that he's the only clever man amongst you. He's got you all on a bit o' string. He goes away, as you mentioned, for a week or ten days together, and never thinks of communicatin' with you; he gets his name in the papers; for all you know he may be playin' a double game—"

The conductor came up for fares, and the argumentative man fortified his position by paying for both.

"A double game. No, no! let me finish! And all the time laughing in his sleeve at the lot of you. I've known that sort before. I've met 'em. I've come across 'em. I say no more," he added mysteriously, and sat back, glaring at the sky.

"Well, but—" The member seemed ill qualified for debate, and Erb was greatly tempted to prompt him. "What I mean is—What I was about to say was—"

"He's a having you," said the other, smiling thoughtfully at the sky, "he's a having you on toast!"

"But what's it to do with you?" demanded the other, not finding the argument for which he had searched.

"Nothing!" retorted the other.

The member, taken aback by this unexpected reply, could not speak for a few moments. He looked appealingly at the names on the shops by which they were passing for a suggestion, and appeared to find one in the word Goodenough.

"After all," he began, "for our purpose—"

"Don't forget this!" interrupted the other. "Don't let this fact slip out of your memory. It was you began this argument. I never seeked for it. We was having a glass in the Old Kent Road, and you, or one of the others, began by saying that Erb was growing a great deal too big for his boots."

"I never said it," growled the other sulkily.

"Did someone pass a remark to that effect, or did someone not pass a remark to that effect? Am I speaking the truth, or am I a bloomin' liar?"

"It's one or the other," said the member cautiously.

"That won't do for me," said the non member, now in the sheer enjoyment of cross examination. "I ast you a straightforward question, and if you can't give me a straightforward answer, why, I must draw me own conclusions. That's all." And smiled again mysteriously at the sky.

"Well," replied the other, goaded, "I don't mind going so far as this. Certain things have been said of late at certain depots that I needn't name, and it's all going to be brought up at the meeting to night. Mind you, it mustn't go any further." The other man gave a nod intended to signify that he had guessed all this. "And being meself on Erb's side, and not wanting to be mixed up in anything like a shindy, why, I'm giving it a miss, and I'm off down to meet the wife's brother at his club in Peckham and spend a nice, quiet, sociable evening. See?"

"And you," remarked the other thoughtfully, "you call yourself a man? Well, well, well!" with a sigh, "the longer we live the older we get."

"What are you snacking at me about now?" demanded the member heatedly.

Erb slipped down the steps, disturbed by the news which he had heard, but with also a feeling of elation at the prospect of a fight. He found the Professor alone in the house in Southampton Street; Rosalind was out giving lessons at a school for superior young ladies at Brixton. Professor full of a kind of stale enthusiasm concerning a new project, which was to take a theatre or a town hall or a room or something and give costume recitals, grave and gay, and to keep on at it night after night until people found themselves forced to come in their thousands; the Professor seemed to have worked this out as though it were a scheme for winning gold at Monte Carlo, and he had already decided what he should do with the enormous profits. Difficulty was to select from the many suburbs of London one place which should be favoured with the experiment; another difficulty (but this he seemed to think of less importance) consisted in the fact that, from inquiries he had caused to be made, it appeared that those who controlled the letting of public premises had a distrustful habit of requiring the rent in advance. Erb, in answer to a question, declared that he had no sort of influence in the City, a place with which the Professor seemed imperfectly acquainted in that he regarded it as a storehouse of valuables, the door of which flew open if you but knew the one, the indispensable word; the Professor considered the matter for a while with one hand twirling his hair, and then, illuminated, announced his intention of taking off his coat to the work. As a first step, he proposed to take a cab to Throgmorton Street, and have a thoroughly good look round. Erb suggested a 'bus and the Professor replied that undertakings of this kind had to be carried through with a certain amount of dash and spirit which could not be done under one and six, or, at the very least, one and three. For this sum Erb compounded, and the Professor made a note of the amount on the back of an envelope that a treacherous memory should not play tricks; the message for Rosalind he could trust to his mind. He was working like a bonded slave, he added, on behalf of his little girl: she was fortunate, indeed, in having a father who could keep accounts. Erb restrained an obvious repartee, and the old gentleman, in his slippers, walked with him out to Camberwell Gate, where, in the interests of economy, he proposed to look in at a bar which had in its window a card bearing the ambiguous announcement, "The 'Stage' Taken In."

Erb found that he had allowed the garrulous old gentleman to detain him longer than he should have done; when, on reaching the coffee shop in Grange Road he ran upstairs to the committee rooms, he could hear voices raised, and he knew that not only had the meeting already commenced, but that a contentious subject was being debated. The rapping of Payne's hammer failed to arrest tumultuous speech, and it was only when Erb opened the door that the argumentative voices stopped.

"Fact of the matter is," said Payne, in the chair, rather hurriedly—"good evening, Erb, you're lateish—the fact of the matter is this is one of them very peculiar subjects where there's something, no doubt, to be said on both sides. Let's get on to the next business."

Erb went to his chair by the side of Payne and took some papers from his pocket. He looked up and down the table nodding; his salutation was not in every case returned, and some of the men glared sternly at the advertisements; Spanswick waved his hand in the friendliest manner.

"There's the matter," said Payne, "the matter of starting a paper or a organ or something of a sim'lar nature. I call upon the secretary to make a statement."

"I object," said a voice.

"That you, Lindsay?"

"Yes, Mr. Chairman," announced a hot faced youth, rising from his seat, "it is me."

"Sed down," advised Spanswick audibly at his side. "Don't make a silly young laughing stock of yourself."

This was sufficient for the fiery faced Mr. Lindsay. He was from St. Pancras, and an engagement with a lady who kept a small laundry at Child's Hill had recently been annulled at her particular request (a circumstance he had related in confidence to everybody), the Midland man having been driving about London for some days boiling up his thoughts, had decided that the world was managed on some erroneous system; it behoved him to put it right. Lindsay had come to the meeting with the vague desire to get satisfaction by opposing something; here in the discussion concerning Erb appeared a subject which exactly fitted his requirements.

"I should like to say a few brief words on the matter which we 'ave jest been discussing."

"Question!" cried Spanswick.

"I'll question you," retorted Lindsay heatedly, "if you can't leave off interruptin'. I appeal to the Midland men present, and I ask whether they're going to allow themselves to be sat upon?"

"You'll be jumped on if you don't look out," said Spanswick. The room began to take sides.

"You do it," shouted the other, goaded. "You do it, that's all! Try it on! Have a dash at it, my friend, and see what 'appens. You talk a lot, but I vurry much doubt whether you can do anything else."

Payne in the chair made his hammer heard above the din of contending voices, and then, standing up, shook the hammer threateningly. If they did not at once stop their row, said Payne, he, as Chairman, would have to consider the advisability of jolly well doing something; having given this vague threat Payne conferred with Erb in a whisper.

"Tell you what occurs to me," said Payne, with a weak pretence of proclaiming an idea of his own. "Let's hear what friend Lindsay has to say, and if there's anything in it, why no doubt our friend the secretary will reply."

"On a point of order—" said Spanswick, rising.

"I should like to point out—" began a Great Western man in the corner.

"Seems to me that the proper course to pursue—" said another.

The Chair hammered away noisily. A half minute of strenuous tumult, and the noise subsided. Lindsay, of St. Pancras, rose, buttoning his jacket; this done he unbuttoned it again, continuing this eccentric action during the whole of his speech. He had some difficulty in finding words at first, but irritating comments from Spanswick served to encourage him, and he succeeded in recapitulating charges which it seemed had been made by certain members, now coy and reserved, against the secretary during the previous half hour; these Lindsay emphasised by a suggestion that friend Barnes was using the society only for his own personal advancement (at this there was a shout of protest from most of the members that made Erb, his gaze fixed on the blank sheet of white foolscap before him, tingle with satisfaction). When having made his fiercest rush, Lindsay, of St. Pancras, showed signs of wavering, it was Spanswick who pricked him again into fury with a banderillo question to another neighbour: "But what was the real reason why the gel wouldn't have him?" asked Spanswick.

Lindsay from St. Pancras, waving his arms excitedly, cried now in a scream that they were paying a princely salary to a man who thought he could twist the society round his little finger; who went about mixing with the nobs and getting his name into the papers; who lorded it over everybody, or tried to; who, to put it briefly, and to put it finally, was trying to push everybody else off the earth. Lindsay begged to move that the secretary, Herbert Barnes, be requested to hand in his resignation without delay.

Lindsay, of St. Pancras, sat down, grumbling to himself in an undertone, his head still shaking with excitement. There was more applause than one would have expected, applause being a thing that can be created furtively by the stamping of feet hidden under the table. Erb rose. As he did so, Spanswick, with his right arm raised, a reminiscence of Board School manners, rose also, and claimed the attention of Payne in the chair.

"I consider it an insult," said Spanswick loudly, "to allow our friend the secretary to answer the ridic'lous attack that has been made upon him. I claim the right to reply on his behalf." Erb sat down. "It's all very well for men to talk who've never been tempted either by the attractions of 'igh society, or—what shall I say—the allurements and what not that titled parties, be they gentlemen or be they ladies, can offer, but put them in our friend Erb's position, and wouldn't they make mistakes the same as he has? Course they would! Besides, there's this to be said—"

Spanswick, going on with elaborate replies to attacks that had never been made, did not look at Erb, preferring to direct his argument to the contumacious Lindsay and his friends: the cheers from Erb's supporters which greeted Spanswick's start diminished in volume as he went on.

"Drop it!" whispered somebody to him. "Drop it, old man, before you spile it."

When Spanswick came to a finish of his ingenious Mark Antony speech the room was left with the impression that charges of a very serious nature had been brought against Erb, and that the principal defence to be urged was the fact of Erb's youth and inexperience. Erb, recognising the damage that Spanswick's advocacy had effected, started up to argue the case from his own point of view, but he was again anticipated by a supporter, this time by a man on whose loyalty he could depend, although his stock of discretion had limits.

"I claim the right to say a few words!" shouted the new man. The room cried, "Erb, Erb, Erb!" being, it seemed, anxious to see if the case could possibly be readjusted, and wishful, at any rate, to see the effort made.

"Take five minutes," ordered the Chair.

"I can do it in under that," said the other generously. "If it's a case of argument by words, I think I'm equal to it: if it's case of argument by fists, I jolly well know I am. Understand that, my fine friend!" he added, addressing Lindsay.

Lindsay of St. Pancras, at a loss for a good repartee, suggested rather wearily that the speaker should go home and fry his face. The room looked on this as wanting in finish, and to Lindsay's confusion gave it no applause.

"You come from St. Pancras, I believe? Very well; I'll St. Pancras you before I've done with you."

"Do it!" cried Lindsay, annoyed by the failure of his retort. "You do it, that's all!"

Lindsay slipped from his seat, and, evading the efforts made by neighbours to detain him, went quickly to the side of the speaker. The Chair half rose, his hammer uplifted. Erb stood up with a pained look.

"Here I am," said Lindsay, offering his scarlet face to Erb's supporter. "Now show us what you can do."

The invitation was one not to be declined. The loud smack on the scarlet face made Lindsay stagger; the next moment he had seized a wooden chair, and the speaker had similarly armed himself. Voices in the room shouted, Payne hammered on the table before him, everybody, in an excited way, begged everybody else to keep calm. Erb made his way, thrusting aside the intervening arm, to the quarter of the room where the two men were facing each other. Lindsay swung his chair, and the other guarded; the two chairs broke noisily, and left the two disputants holding a single wooden leg. Spanswick remarked that Lindsay seemed about as successful in undertakings of this kind as in his love affairs, and the St. Pancras youth, goaded by this, brought the leg of the chair viciously down on the head of his opponent. A red line matted the hair; the room filled with uproar.

"Stop 'em! Keep 'em apart!"

"Let 'em fight it out! Stand back and let 'em finish it!"

"Leave off shoving me then! I've got as good a right to look on as you have. For two pins—"

"The other one began it. He asked for it."

"I beg your pardon, he did nothing of the kind whatsoever. Keep your elbows out of the way, or else I'll serve you like he served him. Yes, and quick about it, too!"

The sight of blood excited all to the point of ill temper. Two, with the best intentions, held Erb firmly, screaming to him urgent recommendations to keep cool, and as Erb was the only man in the room capable of exercising any control over the members, there seemed no reason why the disturbance should not go on for all time; the arrival of the landlord with a threat of police caused the two men to loosen their hold of Erb, and he, with a fierce remark condemning the stupidity of all, freed himself, and took charge of the proceedings. Ordered Payne to turn the landlord out and lock the door. Directed his supporters to resume their seats. Found the decanter, the contents of which had been only partly upset, and, pouring water into the palm of his hand, bathed the damaged man's head. Commanded Lindsay to stand away at the end of the room by himself, which that young man did, to his own astonishment, in the manner of a penitent schoolboy. Gave orders to members of one or two disputant groups, causing them to separate and occupy themselves with other duties. Whispered to Payne. Payne went back to his chair and his hammer.

"Friends," cried Payne, mopping his forehead, "this meeting's going to be adjourned for 'alf a hower so as to get cool."

Most of the men went downstairs, and in the bar discussed the tumultuous event with hushed voices, that outsiders might not share the knowledge; they were not quite certain whether to be proud of the incident or ashamed. Erb told off two men to take his damaged advocate to a chemist's, and, giving no answer to inquiries concerning his intentions, went out, and walked up and down Grange Road alone. He saw the whole case clearly; admitted that his popularity had received a shock; recognised the true inwardness of Spanswick's intervention, and foresaw the difficulties that would obstruct his path if he should lose his position. Not seeing Rosalind this evening was, he now felt, an augury of bad luck; he would be glad when the night was over and done with.

"This ain't my birthday," said Erb grimly.

All the same, something had to be done. Individual men one could deal with, but with men in a lump you could only safely count on their unreliability. Erb stopped at a furniture shop and tried to guess the identity of a young man with hat tipped back and forehead creased with thought; the face looked familiar, and it was only on approaching that he discovered it was his own reflection in a long mirror marked in chalk, "A Rare Bargain. Late the Property of a Club." He laughed and went back.

"I don't want to make a speech," he said quietly. The room had refilled, members conducting themselves with a studied decorum almost painful to behold; the smoke had escaped by the open windows, and it was possible to see everything clearly. "It appears that there's some dissatisfaction."

"No, no!" said voices.

"There's some dissatisfaction," repeated Erb determinedly, "and it doesn't really matter much whether it's grounded or not. No society can go on like this with success under these circumstances. I started this society—"

"Earear!"

"And I tell you candidly, I feel much more interested in the prosperity of this society than I do in the prosperity of myself. I'm a single man, I regret to—I mean to say I'm a single man, and as a single man, I can find something else to do."

Members looked at each other with concern.

"That is why, Mr. Chairman, I address myself to you, because you're an old friend and a—and a good sort." Payne blinked at the compliment. "And I hand to you, old chum, this letter that I've just written out, which contains—"

The room leaned forward to listen.

"Contains my resignation." Erb sat down.

A murmur started slowly near the Chairman and went down the table, increased its pace and its volume, and came back to Erb in the condition of an angry remonstrance. Half a dozen men rose.

"I give notice," said Spanswick, "that at the next meeting I shall move the appointment of a new secretary."

"At the next meeting," said a Cannon Street man, who had never heard his own voice raised in public speech before, and seemed himself astonished by the novelty, "at the next meeting you'll damn well do nothing of the kind." The room roared its approval. "We don't want a new secretary, because we ain't a going to get rid of the old one. The position isn't vacant. I move, Mr. Chairman, or second, or whatever you call it, that that letter what you've got in your hand be given back to our friend Erb, and that he be asked or invited or requested—I don't know how you put these things—to tear it up and forget all about it; I will now conclude my few remarks by asking you to join me in a well known song."

"F—or he's a jolly good faillow, For he's—"

The room sang the refrain with enthusiasm; the man with the broken head came, bandaged, and joined in. Spanswick, recognising that the game for the present was over, beat time.

"That's all right, then," said Payne, when the hurrahing stopped. "Now, let's get on to the next business. 'Proposed starting of a new paper to be called "The Carman."'"

CHAPTER XII

The incident revealed to Erb the fact that the men's support and confidence had something of a tidal nature. He had watched, sometimes with amusement, always with interest, the state of other leaders—from high water, when they could swim luxuriously, to low water, when they were left stranded ludicrously on the beach; it had not before occurred to him that he himself might encounter a similar experience; he determined now to make his position as secure as possible. In this effort he relied a good deal on the new journal he was preparing, the first number of which was to bear on the front page the words, "Edited by Herbert C. Barnes." Lady Frances had written on the subject of labour—

"Oh horny handed sons of toil, Who spin and weave and dig in mines."

Erb, summoned to Eaton Square to take charge of this (the risk of loss in the post being too great to endure), had ventured to point out to the poetess, with, of course, great respect, that it would have been more appropriate to introduce something about kindness to horses and the difficulties occasioned by the stress and turmoil of traffic; Lady Frances, listening with a slight frown on her young forehead, answered that she was much obliged, that she thought she saw her way to another poem to be called "Sturm and Drang," but she felt it would be unwise to touch the first effort; good poetry was always dashed off on the impulse of the moment.

"I didn't know that," remarked Erb, with deference.

So poem Number One was to go in, please, exactly as she had written it, and on the day the paper came out would Erb oblige her very much by coming to dinner at Eaton Square.

"Dinner?" echoed Erb amazedly.

Coming to dinner at Eaton Square, and bringing with him one, or perhaps more, copies.

"What about an evening suit, Lady Frances?"

The managerial young woman had thought of that; her uncle and a few more men would be present, and, to make the dinner quite informal, they would wear morning dress. No, no, please, no excuses of any kind. Lady Frances was going to see her tailor in Maddox Street, and she could give Erb a lift so far. The tall maid (who was Miss Luker of the dance) being rung for, brought in hat and cloak, and helped her young mistress with them, giving no glance towards Erb, and the two went downstairs together. Seated at the side of Lady Frances, he was watched curiously by the drivers of one or two railway vans, who, in their anxiety to verify what appeared to be a dream, looked round by the side, allowing thus their blinkered horses to peer into omnibuses and nibble at conductors' hats, necessitating a swift exchange of the kind of repartee in which the London driver is a past master. When Erb stepped out at Maddox Street and raising his hat started back to a point whence he could walk to his office at Bermondsey, Erb noticed that Lady Frances had a look on her face that might come to one who advanced the cause of millions and, by an act of her own, had made a whole world glad. It would be quite unfair to suggest that at this period Erb was by way of becoming a snob, but it would be untrue to say that he had any objection to the soft, pleasant scent, the well bred air, the gracious manner that he found with Lady Frances. It is also right to say that directly he had left her he began to think of Rosalind and of his work. At this period sometimes one came first, sometimes the other.

"Dinner!" he said to himself.

"Me at dinner at Eaton Square. 'Pon my life, this is the funniest world I ever saw."

He retained his old habit of talking as he went along the London streets, and people in a hurry stopped on noticing this, and delivered themselves of an opinion in regard to his sanity. In this way he often had long talks with Rosalind of an extremely fervent nature; Rosalind helping him with a few coy questions, all in a way that had never yet found realisation; his fluency in these rehearsals astonished him sometimes as much as his inexcusable awkwardness when he called at Camberwell.

"I'm a bit of a muddler," he confessed in Waterloo Place, "where women are concerned. In other matters, now—Look where you're coming, stupid!"

Spanswick, red faced, short necked, and pimpled, addressed in this way, was walking backwards in the inconvenient manner adopted by some on crowded pavements who wish to review scenes that have passed; it was a silken ankle stepping into a carriage that had clipped Spanswick's attention.

"What ho!" cried Spanswick. "Still a lordin' it, Erb, old man? Kind of a amphibious animal, ain't you?"

"I can swim!" said Erb.

"The best swimmers get drownded sometimes."

"Not more than once."

"Talking of which," said Spanswick cheerily, "are you going to stand us a drink?"

"No," replied Erb.

"Ah, well," said Spanswick with an effort, "me and you can't afford to quarrel. We've both got our axes to grind. Whereabouts is Pall Mall?"

"You're in it now. It runs up that way to the bottom of St. James's Street."

"That's the best of 'aving been a parcels carman," sighed Spanswick enviously. "I was never anything but a goods man, and I never had no chances of getting amongst the aristocracy as you have. Otherwise I should meet you on equal terms. How's the young woman?"

"What young woman?"

"Are there so many of 'em as all that? Seems to me," remarked Spanswick thoughtfully, "that some of you lead a double life. You'll come a cropper over it some day, mark my words."

"I'll mark your face," retorted Erb with a sudden burst of annoyance. "I've put up with just about enough from you. I may be your secretary, but I'm not your slave."

"Old man, don't let's go kicking up a common fracass here. You don't understand my style of humour. This newspaper, or journal, or organ, or whatever you like to call it—how's it going?"

"Well," said Erb, returning to good temper. "I find I'm having to do it pretty nigh all myself. There's another column to do now before the first number's ready."

"I'm pretty 'andy with me pen," remarked the other. "I don't prefess to be a literary man, of course, but—I'll send you in a few items of news."

"I shall be ever so much obliged to you. Make 'em smart and readable, mind."

"I'll make 'em smart," said Spanswick.

It seemed to Erb, on the day "The Carman" was to appear, that something special of a less selfish character than the dinner in Eaton Square should be arranged to mark the event. What he vaguely desired was to give an outing to Louisa—the short sister had become too weak to take public promenade, and the current young man had to shout to her of an evening, gripping the railings in Page's Walk. Erb had some daring thought of inviting Rosalind, and taking them both up the river. This detail of the plan he accepted and rejected, and accepted and rejected again; meeting Rosalind herself one evening in the strenuous fight for trams on the Surrey side of Blackfriars Bridge, he, after protecting her in the struggle up the steps, and allowing himself in the carrying out of his duty to press the plump arm above the elbow, found himself in the mood of accepting the detail, and he submitted the proposal in a way meant to be deferential, which, however, came out quite brusque and defiant. "Ever been to Battersea Park?" he asked gruffly. Rosalind had never been to Battersea Park. "Care to go?" Rosalind was so busy that she feared—"I'm going to take Louisa." In that case (with a flush that went partly over her face and then ran away), in that case Rosalind would be very pleased. "Must be Wednesday next," said Erb shortly. Wednesday was rather an awkward day, because there was a pupil at half past one, who came in her dinner hour, and another at three. "Put her off," commanded Erb. Very well, then, the three o'clock pupil should be off; Rosalind declared she would be thinking of the afternoon every hour of the day until it arrived. "So shall I," said Erb shortly. Had Erb seen Lady Frances lately? "We can't bear to be apart," said Erb, in a tone meant to be jocular.

There were times when the one thing certain seemed to be that by no possible chance could the first number of "The Carman" come out on the day appointed. The printers did not place the importance of the undertaking so high as Erb did; difficult to make them understand the importance of producing it on the day fixed; the foreman of the noisy, rattling printing establishment in Southwark said frankly that the world having done without the journal for so long, no great hurt could be occasioned if it should be a day or two late.

But on the day, their van drove up to the doorway of the office where Erb and some of the committee were waiting, and a minute later each man had a copy in his hands, his eyes fixed on the gratifying place where his own name appeared. Erb had taken ingenious care to mention as many names as possible, and, because of this, railway vans sent, say, from Paddington to Haverstock Hill, made a slight detour and called at Bermondsey for copies. There were some misprints, and one man, whose Christian name was given as John instead of James, cancelled his subscription instantly, and prophesied a gloomy future for the paper. Erb demanded opinions, and discovered to his regret, that nearly every line in the small paper received condemnation from somebody (personal paragraphs about high officials in the railway world alone excepted), the fact being that the readers of "The Carman" misapprehended the question, and assumed, when asked for an opinion, that they were invited to give adverse judgment; a thing that has happened with other critics in other circumstances.

But the particular copies presented to Louisa and to Rosalind extorted from these young women, on their way slowly to Cherry Garden Pier, unqualified approval. On the pier, where they waited for the steamer coming up from Greenwich, the two ladies read again the printed references to themselves.

"Yours," said Erb importantly, fanning himself with his straw hat, "yours is what we newspaper people call a dummy ad."

"I can pay for mine," said Rosalind quickly.

"You'll do nothing of the sort," retorted Erb. "Read it out!"

She read it with a flush of gratification on her young face, Erb looking over her shoulder. The scent of brown Windsor came to him.

"'Miss Rosalind Danks,'" she read, "'Professor of Elocution, Declamation, Gesture, et cetera, et cetera. Number so and so Southampton Street, Camberwell, S.E. Schools attended. Private lessons given. Assisted by Mr. Reginald C. Danks, formerly of the principal West End theatres. "We shall never forget his Montgiron."—Vide Press.'"

"Now yours, Louisa."

A break in his short sister's voice betokened uncontrollable pride.

"'We are glad to say that Miss L. Barnes, younger sister of our secretary, is slowly recovering from a rather serious illness.' First time," said Louisa, waving the journal in the air, "the very first time my name's ever been in print."

"May I suggest, Mr. Editor," said Rosalind, leading him to the iron chain that protected the edge of the pier, "that it is a little clumsy to express satisfaction at slow recovery? It wasn't what you meant."

"Don't let on to her about it," urged Erb distressed. "I haven't got quite the hang of writing. Is there anything else you noticed?"

"Nothing of importance."

"Tell us," begged the anxious editor, "and get it over."

"These personal paragraphs, headed 'What we Want to Know.'"

"The men all liked them."

"A little spiteful," she said quietly. "Calculated to hurt somebody. I shouldn't, if I were you. This one, for instance."

"We'll drop 'em in number two. Here's our boat coming."

Some particular people complain of the river steamers, but the "Flying Arrow" that took charge of the three at London Bridge, and conveyed them up under railway bridges, and past embankments, and by the terrace of the House of Commons—Erb waved his straw hat to his friend the white haired labour member, and the labour member waved in return in such a friendly manner that other passengers became at once interested in Erb, and whispered (to Louisa's great satisfaction), "Who is he? Who is he, eh?"—by the Tate Gallery, and between unattractive stores, Nine Elms way, the "Flying Arrow," I say, for these three young people might have been a gaily caparisoned barge lent by Cleopatra; the gramophone that squeaked out songs in a ghostly, unnatural tone of voice, a selected troupe from the Royal Italian

Opera; and the changes that the atmosphere took from inexpensive cigars and cheap tobaccos, the choicest perfumes from Old Bond Street. The top note of satisfaction was reached when Erb, invited to political debate by the self confident captain, worsted that uniformed official with the greatest possible ease, and sent him back limp to the bridge, to resume a profession for which he was qualified. Disappointing, perhaps, to find that people on the steamboat who studied literature were not applying themselves to "The Carman," devoting their minds, instead, to cheap journals, which offered German pictures (second hand), with American jokes underneath, not absolutely new. Erb left two copies of "The Carman," one aft and one at the other end, and the girls watched results; a lad with a bulgy forehead took up a copy and read it with languid interest; he presently dropped it on the deck, and a waiter in a bowler hat who came along at that moment threw it into the river, where it drifted away helplessly. The other copy seemed likely to taste more of success, for a woman seized it with every sign of delight; when she proceeded to wrap up a pair of boots in the new journal Erb felt annoyed. But it was not easy to remain in this state with a cheerful young woman like Louisa, or with a more sedate but equally agreeable person like Rosalind, and they presently had a great game of pretending that they were royalty on a tour round the world, so that Nine Elms pier became Gibraltar, and a few minutes later they were going through the Suez Canal, which others called Battersea Bridge. On reaching Sydney (which had no harbour to speak of, but possessed a wobbling pier marked Battersea Park) they disembarked with most of the other voyagers, some of whom had decided that the three were either theatrical people or not quite right in their heads. As they went up the wooden gangway and entered the Park, Louisa had colour in her white cheeks, and, declining assistance of her companions, ordered them to give each other their arms. Which they did for a moment only.

"Shan't go to that dinner this evening," said Erb.

"I think you will," remarked Rosalind.

"Catch you," said Louisa satirically, "catch you missing a chance like that."

"I shan't go. I don't want anything better'n this."

"You'll have to," decided Louisa. "And come back and tell us all about it. I'd give anything to see Alice's face when she hears you've been upstairs."

"I'd forgot about Alice."

"She's forgot about us," retorted Louisa. "That's the worst of tall people, they always look down on you. How'd it be if I sat down here for a bit and let you two walk on and come back for me?"

"And leave you alone?" asked Rosalind.

"I can set here and laugh at the foreigners," she remarked.

Erb and Rosalind made Louisa comfortable on a chair, and left her applying herself once more to the intellectual delight of again reading through "The Carman," with special attention to the paragraph that concerned herself. Just before they went out of sight of her, in going round the circle where bicycles were swishing along, they turned and waved their hands: she unpinned her straw hat and lifted it in a gentlemanly way.

"I wonder," said Erb thoughtfully, "whether she's going to make old bones."

"I shouldn't let her go again to that work of hers."

"If anything serious happened," he said slowly, "I'd make such a stir about the business that they'd have to shut up the factory."

"That wouldn't bring her back," remarked Rosalind.

"Back?" Erb stopped affrighted. "Why you don't think—you don't fancy for a moment, do you, that she's going to—" They walked on quickly for a while. "My goodness," he cried excitedly, "I'd tear the place down for them! There shouldn't be a stone left! I'd get questions asked about the business in Parliament! I'd organise meetings. I'd make London get white hot about it! I'd never let 'em rest. I'd set every society at 'em. We'd get up demonstrations in the streets. We'd—"

"Don't let's get cross about anything," said Rosalind. "I want to look back on to day when I get into my dull moments."

"You never get dull."

"I suppose nobody's life is perfectly happy."

"I say," said Erb, walking nearer to her and speaking in an undertone. "You never worry about that chap Railton, do you?"

"Not—not very often."

"That's right," he said. "You know there's no man in this world that is worth a single tear from your eyes."

"Don't talk about me as though I were perfect."

"You wouldn't be perfect," said Erb, "if it wasn't for your faults."

They talked of Louisa, and reckoned up amusedly her long list of engagements. From this Erb went on to a short lecture on the time that some wasted over affairs of the heart, urging that there were other matters of equal or greater interest in life, such as the joy of getting on better than other people, and thus extorting the open envy, the cloaked admiration of colleagues. He succeeded at last in minimising the value of love to such a small amount that his companion ceased to give any consenting words, and, noticing her silence, he recognised that he was outrunning her approval; he had to hark back to the point where her silence had commenced to hint at want of agreement. They read the wooden labels on preposterous looking trees, and invented names of like manner for themselves: Erb delivered a brief address from the banks of the lake to the swans on the water, urging them to form a society of their own and to fight to the last feather for their rights: they found a long broad avenue under trees that leaned across at the top, and a perfectly new Rosalind offered, in a sportive way that amazed Erb and gratified him, to race him as far as a mail cart, and Erb starting, took no trouble over what appeared an easy task, with the result that he reached the winning post badly beaten by the limping girl by several yards, and forced to endure from the baby occupant of a mail cart a sneer of contempt. They rested after this, and, whilst Erb fanned her with his copy of "The Carman," Rosalind talked of her father, and, instead of becoming serious as usual when the old Professor occupied her thoughts, told with great enjoyment the story of a great week once at Littlehampton when they were playing "East Lynne" with a fit up company to such imperfectly filled houses that it became certain there would be not only no money with which to pay the excellent landlady on Sunday morning, but scarce a penny to buy food on Saturday. Of aforesaid excellent landlady coming in on the Saturday night and making one of eight people in the pit, and being so affected by the performance by Rosalind as little Willy, and moved to such anguish of tears by the scene, that she bustled out between the last acts, purchased a sheep's head at the butcher's, had a fragrant, gorgeous supper ready for the Professor and Rosalind on their hungry return, and came in after the meal, when the two had searched once more for an emergency exit from the situation, with formal announcement to the effect that she knew quite well that they hadn't a shilling to bless themselves with, that her native town in regard to appreciation of the dramatic art was past praying for; that Rosalind was a little dear, and that, for her part, if she touched a copper of their non existent money she would never again know a moment's peace: the landlady begged two favours, and two favours only—first, that she might give the little girl a good hug; second, that she might be permitted to stay up and bake them a meat and potato pie that would keep their bodies and souls together on to morrow's journey.

They remembered Louisa presently, and went back to the white faced girl, who had found company in a penny novelette left on the seat by someone tired of literature, and who made them go away again until she ascertained whether the young woman in the story married the brilliant young journalist or the middle aged Peer. When justice had been done by presentation of the prize to brains, and the House of Lords, resigning itself without a murmur, had given its blessing and a cheque, she called them back, and the three held council in regard to the dinner in Eaton Square. Erb was still inclined to be obstinate, but the two young women were equally determined, and they took him across the bridge into King's Road, where the committee purchased for him a new neck tie, the while they sent him away to wash his face and hands. They left him presently at Sloane Square, and went home to Bermondsey, because Louisa was now forced to confess that she had become tired; Rosalind having the evening free, and being anxious to hear the report of Erb's experience in Eaton Square, offered to read to her in Page's Walk.

Events progressed in Page's Walk to the point of a cozy chat, where Louisa defied sleep in order to recite to Rosalind in their due order the circumstances of the many engagements from the respective starts to the individual finishes, with imitations of the voice of each suitor, and occasionally a parody of the gait. It was in the middle of a diverting account of Number Five—who had at least one defect in that he had no roof to his mouth—that Erb returned. The two surrounded him, firing questions.

"One at a time," said Erb, good humoured, because of the unexpected joy of seeing Rosalind again. "One at a time. There were small things first, sardines and what not—"

"Hors d'œuvres," said Rosalind.

"I daresay. Anyhow, after that, soup."

"Can't stand soup," remarked Louisa. "There's no stay in soup. Go on, Erb."

"Now comes what I may term," said Erb, "the gist or point of this anecdote. The lady with the shoulders next to me—"

"I should faint if I found myself going out like that," declared Louisa, interrupting again. "How anyone can do it beats me. It's like being caught in your disables."

"The lady with the shoulders next to me turned and asked me something that I didn't exactly catch, and I turned round rather suddenly and said, 'Beg pardon?' Knocked the arm of the girl who was serving the fish, and as near upset the plate that she held in her hand as didn't matter. I jumps up, and then for the first time I recognised it was Alice."

"Wasn't she took aback?"

"Not half so much as I was," said Erb. "I suppose being rather a large dinner party they'd laid her on extra. Of course, I shook hands with her and said, 'Hullo, Alice, how's the world using you?'"

"Well, you are," said Louisa with horror, "absolutely the biggest juggins I ever come across."

"But what was I to do?"

"Do?" echoed the short sister. "Do? I could have soon shown you what to do. All you'd got to do was to take no notice of her. Ignore her! Look past her! Pretend she wasn't there! You'll never get asked again, that's a very sure thing."

"I don't care," answered Erb. "I'm an awkward chap in these West End circles. When I'm not in 'em I want to be there, and once I'm there I look round directly for an open door to slip out of."

"And what did Miss Alice have to say for herself?" asked Louisa, coming back to the incident with relish.

"Oh, she kept very cool, and she just whispered, 'Sit down, Erb, and behave.'"

"That's her all over."

"They stared at me naturally enough, and young Lady Frances seemed a bit upset just for a moment, and nobody spoke for a bit, but after a while they were all chatting away again, and the party with the shoulders next to me began asking me what I thought of the new woman at Covent Garden. Then I put me foot in it again," said Erb amusedly. "I thought she meant the market."

"How they'd pull you to pieces after you left," remarked Louisa sighing. "I can 'ear 'em saying things."

"I can't," said Erb contentedly. "And if I did I shouldn't care. What would you have done," he appealed to Rosalind, "what would you have done, now, in similar circumstances?"

Rosalind, as she put on her gloves, considered for a moment before replying. Then she leaned towards him and touched Erb's knee lightly.

"I should have done," she said, "exactly as you did."

There were several reasons why Erb should not take her by the arms; all these reasons jumped up before him as he rose and made a step forward. He stopped himself with an effort, and preceded her to the door. They went downstairs, and he walked bareheaded as far as the "Lord Nelson."

"You were never nearer being kissed," he said to her ear, "in all your life."

"Please, please," she said reprovingly.

Erb went back to Page's Walk checked and cooled by this reproof. The prospect that he had had momentarily in his mind of the small house close to Wandsworth Common, with a billiard table lawn at the back, at a time when he, perhaps, would be in the House, unique among all labour members by reason of having a wife who could be introduced with confidence, was dismissed with a caution.

"Letter for you, Erb, on the mantel," cried Louisa from her room. "It's just been sent over. Good night!"

A portentous envelope, addressed to the Editor of "The Carman." Erb sliced it with his penknife. The large letter paper was folded in three.

"SIR,

"We have been consulted by our client, Sir William Durmin, with reference to the libellous statement which appears in No. I of 'The Carman.'

"Our client cannot allow such statements to be made, and our instructions are to issue a writ without further notice.

"If you wish to avoid personal service, please supply us by return of post with the name of your solicitor who will accept service on your behalf.

"Yours faithfully."

"Now," said Erb, "the band's beginning to play."

CHAPTER XIII

If publicity at any cost be a good thing for a new journal, then "The Carman" had no right whatever to complain. The men belonging to the Society felt exultant at references to the impending action. It seemed that they were defying Capital as Capital had never been defied before. They told each other, when they met at receiving offices and railway stations, that Capital was going to have a nasty show up. Erb looked forward to the struggle with eagerness, until he had a meeting with Spanswick, the writer of the paragraph; that amateur journalist admitted, at the end of a keen cross examination, that he had, perhaps, erred in stating that he knew the statement as a fact of his own knowledge: he remembered now that it had been related to him by a chap of his acquaintance, who was either on the Great Eastern or the South Western, he would not swear which, and he confessed to the indignant Erb that he could no more place his hand on this man's shoulders and produce him at the Law Courts "than the dead." Erb told Spanswick exactly what he thought of him, and Spanswick, penitent, declared that it would be a warning for the future: he would not have had this happen for forty thousand pounds. If Erb required him to go into a witness box he would guarantee to say on oath just whatever Erb wished him to say. This sporting offer being declined, Spanswick went with downcast head, and examined the lining of his cap, as though hopeful that some solution of the difficulty would be found there. Once clear of the place he gave on the wooden flags of a cellar in Grange Road a few steps of a dance, which seemed to intimate that his regret was but a cloak that could be discarded without much difficulty.

No easy thing to keep up an attitude of hopefulness before the men whilst searching uselessly for facts to justify the Spanswick paragraph; but this was a mere diversion compared with the trouble that came to him the following week. Louisa was at home again after a few days of work at the factory, and Erb, going one afternoon to Page's Walk for some correspondence, encountered the doctor who had called for a minute to see her. The doctor was a breathless, energetic man, whose fees were so small that, added up, they only made a living wage by reason of the number of his patients.

"Going on all right, doctor?"

"Yes, thanks," replied the medical man, walking rapidly through the passage, and brushing his hat the while. "Busy though! Up to my eyes in work."

"I was referring more particularly to my young sister."

"Oh! she! Oh! it's what might be expected. Hideous occupation, I call it. One of those manufactures that might well be left to foreigners. Good day!"

"One moment," said Erb, placing a hand on the doctor's arm, and speaking with great anxiety. "Tell us exactly what you mean in plain language. Ought she to be sent away again?"

"You don't want to waste money," said the doctor, glancing at his watch.

"If it's necessary for her health, I'd spend the last penny I've got."

"Would you really?" The doctor seemed genuinely surprised. "Well, then, perhaps she might get away to the country or the seaside or somewhere."

"May be the means of saving her life?"

"Oh, no," said the doctor cheerfully. "I wouldn't go so far as that."

Erb shook him violently.

"Why didn't you tell me this before? You—"

"Thought you had the sense to see," said the doctor curtly. "Credited you with more intelligence apparently than you possess. Good day!"

Louisa resting upstairs in the one armchair declared that she had never felt better. It was only that she was tired, and had no appetite; but, then, see what a good thing it was to feel tired, and just imagine what a saving was effected by the absence of a craving for unlimited food! Erb did not tell his sister what the doctor had said, but his grave appearance hinted something, and Louisa declared not only that all doctors were fools, but went further, and asserted that most of them were born fools. All the same, she consented with some reluctance to go away. Erb went down to Camberwell, to see Rosalind and talk it over. At Camberwell, Rosalind, ready dressed for public promenade, came halfway down the uneven pavement and met him, with both hands outstretched, just by Minerva. She had only that moment been speaking of him to the Professor, and the Professor had said that he, for his part, felt a keen desire to see Erb again.

"But we won't see him," she said, in a confidential way that was very pleasing, "because he will only want to borrow, and I am used to his borrowing from most people; but it hurts when he borrows from you."

"We'll talk in the hall," suggested Erb.

"In a whisper," said Rosalind.

The rare good point of talking in a whisper was that they were obliged to place their heads closely together. Erb explained the difficulty, and Rosalind, after considering for a moment, announced the decision in her emphatic way. School holidays would soon be on. She wanted to take a fortnight's holiday herself: she would take Louisa away with her, either to Aunt Emma's, at Penshurst, or, if the seaside was ordered, to Worthing.

"Spoiling your own holiday!"

"Not at all, not at all!" she answered decidedly. "It's going to be, any way."

"But why should you trouble? I could get Lady Frances—she'd do anything for me."

"No doubt! Find my umbrella there in the corner—the one with the silver knob—and walk down with me to the school."

It was certainly very pleasant to see how the young woman, after a few moments of reserve, and in the presence of Erb's depression, became brighter than usual, pushing away all her own trouble, and talking of the Professor's last escapade as though it were the best joke in the world. The Professor, still declining in the service of the profession, had recently been offered the post of baggage man in a newly starting provincial company, with the added duty of acting as understudies to the man who played the old City man in Act I., and the Chief of Police in Russia in Act IV. Professor, with many protestations and frequent appeals to the shades of Barry Sullivan and John Ryder and others, had accepted the offer, and, securing on the Saturday night the sum of ten shillings in advance for the purpose of obtaining fine linen, appeared at St. Pancras station the next afternoon on the starting of the special, and denounced "The Banker's Blood" Company, individually and generally, called upon Heaven to punish them for the attempt to degrade one who had trod the boards long before many of them had been allowed, mistakenly, to see the light of day, and altogether making such a furious scene on the platform, that the manager, consulting hastily with other members of the company in the labelled compartments, gave Rosalind's father another half sovereign to refrain from accompanying the party. All of which Rosalind told in such a merry way that Erb found himself for a time half wooed from melancholy.

"That blessed paper," he said, going back to trouble ruefully, "has got me in a corner the very first start off."

"It wants fifteen minutes to the hour," said Rosalind, looking up at the clock at the corner. "Let's walk round the Green and hear all about it."

Rosalind's hopeful view of the matter was that it might be only what was called a "try on," and the statement of Erb that he felt he hadn't a leg to stand on, she declared to be unworthy of him.

Erb walked back to his office feeling that the talk had done good. It was certainly a great thing to find himself more hopeful in regard to Louisa. But he composed on the way a bitter, bitter paragraph concerning the firm in Neckinger Road and its occupation. This seemed so excellent, that he had half a mind to turn it into poetry, but there proved to be some difficulty in finding rhymes for "murder" and for "dastardly," and he allowed himself on arrival to write it in prose. The copy for number three being made up, he deleted a humorous paragraph about a Bricklayers' Arms man, whose wife had run away, and this made room. There was much in the lines themselves; more to be read by those who could fill up the blank spaces intervening. Erb looked at it when he had crossed the t's and dotted the i's with the pride of a man who, with a mere dip of ink, could force monied folk to tremble. A fine thing to have control in this way over the printed word.

All the more satisfactory to get on a grievance, which appeared to be solid, in that he eventually found that he had to step out apologetically from the corner into which Spanswick's ingenuity had thrust him. There were, it appeared, no grounds whatever for the statement made, and in Featherstone Buildings, Holborn, in a dim office with one light, under which he had to sit, whilst the two partners of the legal firm remained at the other end of the table in the shadow, he underwent, perhaps, the very worst quarter of an hour that he had endured since the time of schooldays. He had had to wait some time whilst one partner was sent for by the other.

"Then we may take it, Mr. Barnes, that you withdraw unreservedly every word of the paragraph in question?"

"That is so."

"And you are prepared to offer every apology and every recompense that is in your power?" asked the other partner.

"I don't know," said Erb, "about recompense."

"Well, then, every apology?"

"I suppose I shall have to taste blacking," he said.

The two partners conferred for a long time in an undertone, the while Erb played nervously with a paper knife. When one of them spoke he held his breath.

"If the paragraph had been copied into other journals, if it had had a wider circulation than that given by your little paper, Mr. Barnes, our client would have instructed us to go on with the legal proceedings, and we should have asked for and obtained heavy damages. If the journal itself was not below contempt—"

"Look here!" interrupted Erb sharply, "don't you go rubbing it in too thick."

"Sir William is a man with a large heart," said the other partner, taking up a more conciliatory tone, "and we shall advise him in the circumstances to do the generous thing. You will print in the next issue of your paper an apology?"

"A most humble apology," remarked the other partner, "terms of which you will permit us to dictate to you. He will not ask you to pay the costs already incurred, and you must think yourself confoundedly—"

"He understands," remarked the second partner. "I am sure Mr. Barnes quite understands. Now let us see about drafting the apology."

"I think I'd better see to that."

"Now, my dear old friend," urged the conciliatory partner.

A most abject apology it was, and the only encouragement for Erb came from the severe partner, who recommended several additions intended to make it of a more cringing nature. Erb signed it after a moment's hesitation, and gave a great sigh of relief when he found himself in Holborn again; he knew that there would be some trouble in convincing his Committee that he had acted throughout with wisdom, but he had so much assurance in his own powers of speech, he had so often taken difficult positions by reason of his own generous ammunition of words, and of their short supply, that he felt confident of success. All the same, the incident would do him no good, and a repetition would undoubtedly weaken his power.

Number Three of "The Carman" came out rather opportunely, for he was able to present a copy to Rosalind and to Louisa on the day he saw them off from London Bridge. They were going to Worthing. Aunt Emma, who had not viewed the sea since childhood's days, was going there from Penshurst in order to ascertain whether it had changed much. Louisa had to be taken to the station in a four wheeler, and as she was helped along by her two companions through a rush of arriving City men, the girl seemed proud of the notice that her white face attracted. Erb recited the stinging paragraph that concerned Louisa's late employers through the open carriage window, when Rosalind had made her patient comfortable with cushions. Two of Louisa's sweethearts, friends in the presence of disaster, stood away against a lamp post, and toyed with automatic machines.

"That's one up against them," said Louisa with relish. She smiled, but the look soon faded.

"If this don't have any effect," declared Erb, "I shall follow it up with something stronger. I'll never let go of 'em."

"Shouldn't like the other gels to lose their shops," remarked Louisa apprehensively.

"But you wouldn't see 'em all get ill like you are?"

"I'm not reely ill," said Louisa. "I'm only pretendin'. Besides, some gels can stand the work and some can't."

"Make her get better," said Erb to Rosalind. "Don't let her have her own way too much."

"Not much use having anyone else's," remarked Louisa, with an effort at the old pertness.

"If she gets up to any of her nonsense send me a telegram."

"I'll write to you very often," said Rosalind quietly. "Let me know—let me know if you see Lady Frances."

The guard cried, "Stand away!" and gave the signal to start. Erb put his head in and kissed his sister's face.

"Might as well serve both alike," suggested Louisa sportively. She rubbed her eyes with her glove.

"Don't dare," said Erb.

One of the infatuated youths walked along with the train, and when Erb, with a wistful look in his eyes, fell back, the youth aimed a packet of chocolate, but either from nervousness or want of practice, missed the compartment and sent it into the next, where four children pounced upon it with a high scream of delight.

The violence of the paragraph concerning the Neckinger Road firm helped to appease those on the Committee who showed uneasiness in regard to what they called the "climb down." True, some of them remarked that the attacks on the Neckinger Road firm had nothing to do with the objects of the society, and Erb, reckoning up, found that he had lost the confidence of three, but a carman who had been discharged by the firm for slight inebriety—"I'm a man that varies," said the ex carman. "Sometimes I may 'ave twenty pints, sometimes I may 'ave thirty pints, and then other days I may 'ave quite a lot,"—came and begged permission to thank them for the public service that the journal was doing, and assured the Committee, with the air of one having exclusive information, that they would get their reward, in this world or in the next, or in both. As the reports from Rosalind at Worthing became less satisfactory, so the fierceness of the attacks in "The Carman" increased; but it was not until a paragraph appeared headed "Wilful Murder!" that Neckinger Road, after taking the previous outbursts with a calm that suggested it was either deaf or asleep, suddenly started up and took action in the most decided and emphatic manner.

Information has been laid this day by for that you, within the district aforesaid, did unlawfully and maliciously publish a certain defamatory libel of and concerning the said well knowing the same defamatory libel to be false, contrary to the statute in such case made and provided. You are therefore hereby summoned to appear before the Court of Summary Jurisdiction sitting at the Southwark Police Court on the twentieth day of October, at the hour of ten in the forenoon, to answer to the said information. Signed with an indistinct signature, one of the magistrates of the police court of the metropolis.

This, on a blue coloured form, which a friendly policeman left one evening, when Erb was wrestling with his brief leading article, and unable to decide whether to give a touch of brightness to the column by the two lines of poetry from William Morris, and risk offending a few subscribers who looked on rhymes as frivolous, or to remain on the safer ground of prose. Erb, in his attacks on the Neckinger Road firm, had begun to feel as a fencer does who makes ingenious passes at the air, and he was so much gratified now to find that he had at last struck something, that he gave the warrant officer something with which to purchase a drink, and had a very friendly chat with him concerning points of law. Erb had to confess he had not hitherto understood—being a man whose mind was occupied with other matters—that one had to appear at a police court in regard to a charge of libel: the warrant officer increased Erb's knowledge by informing him that not only was this the case where no damages were claimed, but that the publication had only to be proved and you were at once committed to the Central Criminal Court to take your trial.

"There," said the officer with relish, "there the Grand Jury has the first go at you, see?"

"They can throw out the Bill?"

"They can," admitted the other grudgingly, "but bless my soul," with a return to cheerfulness, "they won't in your case. Then, in what you may term due course, on comes your case. See? You can either defend yourself—"

"I shall."

"You know the old saying, I s'pose?"

"Never mind the old saying," replied Erb. "Get on!"

"Then, of course, if you're fool enough to conduct your own case, you'll be fool enough to cross examine the witnesses for the other side."

"I shall," said Erb.

"And a fine old mess you'll make of it," remarked the warrant officer, laughing uproariously. "Lord! I'd give an ounce of shag to be in court when it comes off."

"I'll see that it comes off."

"I've seen some of the biggest larks when chaps have been trying to do this sort of thing on their own, that ever you can imagine. Sometimes when I'm a bit down hearted over anything, or if the wife's a bit aggravatin', I just cast my mind back and—"

The warrant officer laughed again, and, taking off his helmet, mopped the inside of it with his handkerchief.

"Never, I suppose," said Erb, a little nettled by this ill timed hilarity, "seen a man in the witness box turned thoroughly inside out?"

"Not by an amateur."

"Never seen him pinned down to certain facts, never watched him being led on and on and on, until he finds that he hasn't got a shred of a reputation, a remnant of a character, not a single white spot of innocence or—"

"I like your talk, old man," interrupted the warrant officer, fixing on his helmet, "and I wish I could stay to hear more of it. But take care you don't wear your face out. So long!"

The police of London are not infallible, but the first prophecies of the warrant officer seemed likely to prove correct. Erb, determined not to fetter himself by legal knowledge, nevertheless found information thrust upon him, and this confirmed the statement that the police court proceedings would be of a simple and formal nature. He regretted the delay, for he was eager to get to close quarters with the firm, and he spent his days in collecting evidence, he walked about at night, always taking in Camberwell in the tour that he might look up at her window, rehearsing the questions that he would put to the firm, imagining contests of words with counsel on the other side, contests from which he always emerged victorious. Spanswick had at last given up all pretence of being a railway carman, and had resigned his membership (this to the relief of Payne and of Erb); it made Erb stop and think for a few minutes, when one afternoon, looking out of his office window he saw Spanswick driving a single horse van belonging to the Neckinger Road firm.

Nothing could be more gratifying than the notice accorded by the evening papers to the hearing at the police court. It happened on a day when little else of importance occurred, so that two journals had the item on their placards—

"ALLEGED NEWSPAPER LIBEL,"

and one of them gave an astonishing portrait of Erb, "Sketched by our Artist in Court," declared the legend underneath, as though this were any excuse. Railway carmen from all quarters somehow managed to include Southwark Police Court in their rounds at the precise hour of the hearing of the case, and when Payne and another householder gave their names in for the purpose of bail they cheered, and the magistrate threatening to have them expelled, they cheered again and filed out at the door.

"Let's have a bloomin' meeting," cried one.

The suggestion clipped their fancy. Erb, coming out quietly, found himself seized by two of the strongest men, carried triumphantly to an empty South Western van standing in Marshalsea Road, and hoisted up to the seat of this, whence, to the obvious surprise of the two roan horses, he made a speech.

"We'll stick to you, Erb," cried some of the crowd.

"Through thick and thin," cried the rest. "Three cheers for Erb. Hip! hip—"

CHAPTER XIV

The weeks had hurried rapidly, more rapidly than usual, for they were pressed with business. The trial at the Central Criminal Court was over, after a hearing that struck Erb as being surprisingly brief, in view of the importance of the case; immediately on the conclusion of the evidence, and the speeches of counsel, the Recorder, from his scarlet cushioned seat, where he had a robed Alderman and a knee breeched Under Sheriff for company, had fined him, courteously and pleasantly, the sum of fifty pounds, or in default two months' imprisonment. The shortness of the trial rendered an organised demonstration of little value in that the men arrived outside the Old Bailey some three hours after the case had been disposed of. Now there is nothing more galling to the Londoner than to be disappointed in his anticipations of a show, and it had required all Erb's tact and more than his usual amiability to appease them.

Erb had expressed a desire to go to prison to purge the offence (a short purgatory in jail was no bad prelude to political life), but the men would not hear of this: they could not manage without him, he was indispensable, they must have someone to look after the society, there was none to take his place, and he had given up this idea with less of reluctance because a disquieting tone had come into the letters of Rosalind from Worthing. But, determined to do something heroic, he insisted that his household goods in Page's Walk should be sold up, and a scene thus contrived that should attract public attention. Wherefore there was an auction room in New Kent Road, to which all the furniture (with the single exception of the bedding) had been removed "For Convenience of Sale," and here were as many of the railway carmen of London as could spare themselves conveniently from their duties, and here also were a few alert eyed youths with note books and sharpened pencils eager to record some incident so amusing that not even a sub editor's pencil should venture to delete. A fusty smell of cocoanut wrappings in the long room, bran new furniture gave an odour of polish, retained and preserved because there was no ventilation except that afforded by the entrance from the street; a good tempered auctioneer at the end of the room, high up and leaning on a rostrum, with a flaring, whistling, naked gas jet that compelled attention, because every now and then it exhibited a humorous desire to singe the top of the auctioneer's shining silk hat. Erb stood by the wall, rather proud of being in the position of a martyr, his men formed a body guard around him. Close up by the auctioneer stood half a dozen decrepit old men, the habitués of the place, ready to snatch up a bargain, to become the intermediaries between buyers and auctioneer, to knock out a sale, or, in short, to do anything and everything except serious labour.

"We have here," said the auctioneer, leaning over his high desk and pointing with his hammer, "a very fine lot—show No. 13, George, and don't be all day about it—a very fine lot, consisting of a pianoforte. Music hath charms, gentlemen, as you know, to soothe the savage breast, and it's always a good investment from that point of view alone. George, jest run over the keys to show these gentlemen what a first class musician you are." The attendant, first rubbing the palm of his hand on his green baize apron, stroked the keys from first note to last. "There!" cried the auctioneer, "there's execution for you! Many a man's been 'anged for less. Now then, what shall we say for this magnificent instrument? Don't all speak at once. Did you say twenty pounds, mister?" This to one of the regulars at the side.

"Not being a blank fool," replied the musty old gentleman, "I did not say twen'y pounds."

"Well! won't anyone say twenty pounds jest for a start? Come now. You've all learnt some language or other."

"Four and six," said one of the carmen chaffingly.

"No, no!" said the auctioneer rather coldly. "I enjoy a joke as well as anyone, but 'pon my word—"

"Five bob!"

"I'm very good tempered," went on the auctioneer, getting red in the face, "and I can stand as much as most men. But—"

"Five and six!"

"Well," with resignation, "have your own way about it. Five and six is offered; five and six in two places; six shillings. I thank you, sir! Who'll say 'alf a sov', eh? Seven shillings! Very well then. But do let's go on a shilling at a time; I can't take sixpenny advances. You know the old story of the girl—"

Erb, looking round with a determined smile on his features, saw Spanswick entering from the pavement; with him a gentleman whose eyes were watery and whose gait was uncertain. Spanswick gave a casual nod to the clump of men, and beckoned to Erb in such an authoritative way that Erb crossed the room when the pianoforte—poor Louisa's pianoforte, that she would allow no one to play—had been knocked down for twenty five shillings. The auctioneer ordered his man to show the horsehair sofa and chairs.

"My friend Doubleday," said Spanswick, introducing his companion. Mr. Doubleday removed his silk hat with care, for the brims seemed rather weak, and in a husky voice declared himself honoured. "One of the cleverest men in South London," whispered Spanswick to Erb, "only he won't recognise the fact. Educated, too!"

"This is a noble action of yours, sir," said Mr. Doubleday, trying to clear his voice. "Reflects the highest credit on what I may venture to term the manhood of South London." Spanswick looked at Erb proudly, as though to say, "He can talk, can't he?" "The newspapers will ring with your praises, sir. Capital will sneak away, abashed and ashamed in the presence of such a brilliant example of self sacrifice and whole hearted devotion. I suppose you haven't got such a thing as a pipe full of tobacco about you? I've come out without my pouch."

"Always comes out without his pouch," remarked Spanswick admiringly.

"No, no!" said Mr. Doubleday, refusing with something of haughtiness Erb's further offer. "I have a match, thank you. I have no desire to be indebted for anything," he drew hard at his pipe, "for anything which I myself possess."

"Independent old beggar, ain't he?" whispered Spanswick.

"My friend here gives me to understand—and I have no doubt that his information is perfectly correct—that you have adopted this attitude because a female relative—a sister, if I mistake not—"

"A sister," admitted Erb.

"Has suffered grievously. Assuming that to be the case, I can only say that I am proud to grasp your hand, sir, and that I desire your acquaintance."

"It ain't many that he'd say that to," whispered Spanswick.

"I want all the friends I've got just now," said Erb.

"The lines of Longfellow," said Mr. Doubleday condescendingly, "spring readily to one's mind." The hammer of the auctioneer went down with a startling crack; something that he said made the group of men laugh, and Erb was called by them to hear it. "We can make our lives sublime, and um tee, umpty, umpty, umpty—footsteps on the sands of time," quoted Mr. Doubleday.

"I must hop off," said Spanswick. "Hasn't he got a marvellous memory?"

"You'll take your friend with you?" said Erb.

"No," said Spanswick, rather awkwardly, "I'll leave him. Fancy he's got something to say to you."

When the sale was over, it occurred to Erb that he had not eaten that day, and as the men had to hurry off to their duties, he would have been left alone but for Mr. Doubleday's presence. Erb was glad to leave the gas scented auction rooms, and would have been content with no other company but his own; he had been acting in a hot, tempestuous way of late, and he was anxious, now that this business was over, to review it all calmly. Anxious, also, think of Louisa, and—But Mr. Doubleday stuck to him, and when Erb entered the Enterprise Dining Rooms, in New Kent Road, Doubleday followed him to the pew, and sat down opposite. Erb gave his order to the girl, who rested the palms of her red hands on the table; when she turned to the other, Doubleday said, assuming the manner of a complaisant guest, that he would have the same.

"Fate," he said, hanging the deplorable silk hat on a wooden peg, "Fate has thrown us together, sir, in a most remarkable way."

"Thought it was Spanswick," said Erb.

"Most inscrutable, the workings of Providence. Stagger even me at times."

"You don't mean that?" said Erb.

"Positive truth!" declared Mr. Doubleday. "Now this meeting with you, for instance. If it had been planned it couldn't have happened more fortunately. Because I have information to give you of the very highest possible value. It means, my dear sir, an absolute epoch making event in your life, and—Ah! roast beef and Yorkshire pudding! Reminds me of my young days. I recollect when I was a bit of a boy—"

Mr. Doubleday, with heavy jest and leaden footed reminiscence, took the duty of conversation upon himself, evidently feeling that he was a bright, diverting companion, one who just for his exceptional powers as a raconteur well deserved to be asked out to dine. His stories were so long, and the telling of them so complicated, that Erb was able to allow his mind to concentrate itself on his own affairs. He had taken a definite, a desperate step; the reaction was setting in, and he began to wonder whether he had been precisely right. Something to feel that whatever he did, right or wrong, he had the solid, obstinate, unreasoning support of the men; one could, of course, count upon this; the greater the misfortune he encountered, the more faithful and obedient would they become. There could be no doubt about that. Besides, they had no one else to guide them. He was, as they had admitted, the one, the necessary man. Any signs of rebellion in the past he had always been able to quell with very little trouble; as a last resource, there was always the threat of resignation. So that was satisfactory enough. Less grateful to remember that the revenge he had tried to take on the Neckinger Road firm had done his sister's health no good whatever. He would run down to Worthing soon to see her and to cheer her.

"Joking apart," said Mr. Doubleday, snapping his finger and thumb to secure the attention of the waitress, "let's come to business. (Cabinet pudding, my dear! I daresay my genial host will take the same.) You must understand, please, that what I am about to submit to you is, as we say in the law, entirely without prejudice."

"Are you a lawyer?"

"I used to be in a secondhand bookseller's. Now, I suppose I'm right in assuming that you could, if necessary, place your hands on a certain sum of money?"

"I could."

"About how much shall we say?" asked Mr. Doubleday engagingly.

Erb counted the money in his pocket.

"Twelve shillings and ninepence."

"I appreciate the humour of that remark," said Mr. Doubleday in his husky voice, "but I want to talk business. I'm a plain, straightforward man, and what I want to know is simply this. Is there a five pound note flying about?"

"If there was," said Erb, "I should catch it."

"There's the benefit money," said the other, looking at himself curiously in the hollow of a spoon, "the benefit money to borrow from, and Yes, yes! I know what you are going to say and I quite agree with you. I think you're most decidedly in the right. Far be it from me to suggest for a single moment—"

"I'm getting tired of you," interrupted Erb suddenly. "I wish you'd take your hook and go away. Your face worries me, and your talk makes my head ache."

"Then it's time I came to close quarters. Listen to me!" Mr. Doubleday leaned his elbows on the table, and, bending forward, shielded his mouth with his hand that words might not go astray. "This is the situation. A man, a young man, takes up a certain high minded attitude in regard to a certain firm; gets hauled up for libel; gets fined. His society comes to his rescue. Newspapers have paragraphs applauding him. So far, so good! Fine thing to show up, as far as he can, dangerous trades. But he forgets or he pretends to forget, doesn't matter which—that not so long ago he, this same young man, went all over the country, making speeches in favour of a syndicate that called itself something or other—"

"I don't ask your permission before I open my mouth," cried Erb heatedly.

"True, my lad, true! You can go further than that. You can say that you didn't do so without being adequately bribed to do it."

"Bribed!" Erb rose at the table and clenched his fist.

"Keep cool!" said Mr. Doubleday, making a military tent of his two hands. "There's no extra charge for sitting down."

"Let me know what you mean by saying that I've been bribed."

"I should have thought that you would have known the meaning of the term by this time. B r i b e is a word meaning the sum accepted for doing work that you had no business to do. We can easily verify it." He snapped his fingers. "Got a dictionary, my dear?"

"To eat?" asked the waitress.

"A dictionary," he repeated with impatience.

"We've got an old London directory."

"Never mind about the exact definition of the word," said Erb steadily. "Tell me at once what you mean by your accusation."

"Have you ever in all your life seen a cheque for twenty pounds?"

"Yes!"

"Made payable to yourself?"

"Yes!"

"And signed by—"

"Yes, yes, go on."

"Nothing more to say," remarked Mr. Doubleday. "There's an end of the matter. Only it's rather a pretty circumstance altogether, don't you think? This self sacrificing chap who has allowed himself to be sold up publicly as a protest against harmful trades, is the same man who earlier in the year was speaking throughout the length and breadth of the land in support of trade infinitely more harmful than the one carried on in Neckinger Road. And," here Mr. Doubleday took down his elderly silk hat and made elaborate pretence of smoothing the nap, "getting uncommonly well paid for it, too. Pretty situation, isn't it?"

"There's a very good answer to the charge you bring against me," said Erb, trying to keep his temper, "but there's no earthly reason why I should give it. I'm not responsible to you; I am responsible to my society."

"Ah," cried Mr. Doubleday, putting his hat on jauntily, "glad you recognise that."

"I do recognise it."

"And having recognised it, you see that it would be very much to your interest that the unfortunate transaction should be kept dark."

"Not at all!"

"In which case," here he stood up ready to go, and slapped his foot with his bamboo cane, "in which case you'd better come, my lad, to this place"—he placed a worn and travelled card with two addresses ruled out and a third written in, "before six o'clock to night. Before six o'clock, mind. A minute past will be too late. And—er—bring that five pound note along with you."

He walked jauntily up the aisle of the dining rooms to the street door; when the waitress flew after him, he whispered a few words and pointed back at Erb with his cane.

"Is that right?" demanded the waitress breathlessly of Erb, "is that right that you pay?"

"Looks like it!" replied Erb moodily.

The threat did good in one way in that it aroused all his fighting instincts and that it diverted his mind from Worthing. Going down Walworth Road to look at Rosalind's house, he rehearsed the expected scene, striking the palm of one hand with the fist the other, and scoring with great neatness over Spanswick and other opponents. Women at the stalls stopped in their loud declaration of the admirable character of their goods, to watch the excited young man as he went by, and remarked to each other that he was evidently in love; an excuse that in their eyes justified any and every sign of eccentric behaviour. On the way back (after walking up and down near the garden of monumental statuary and glancing shyly each time at her window), he met the Professor, and for the sheer pleasure of talking of her engaged him in conversation. The Professor deplored the fact that after you had given the best years of your life to the education of an only child, she should go off to the seaside for a holiday without so much as thinking for a moment of taking you with her, and asked Erb whether he had half a crown about him in exchange for two separate shillings and a sixpence. On Erb producing this coin the Professor found, with many expressions of deep regret, that he had left the smaller pieces in a waistcoat at home.

"But I shan't forget, my dear chap," said the Professor, raising his hand for a stage clasp. "I am one of those who never permit a kindness to escape from their memory. But I hate to be badgered. That ungrateful young scamp Railton, for instance."

"Ah!"

"What have I not done, or rather what have I not promised to do, for him."

"Daresay! But—"

"Engaged at one time to my accomplished daughter."

"But what about him?"

"I am not romancing," said the other impressively. "I am simply giving you the downright, honest, blunt, straightforward truth when I tell you that he wrote this morning asking me for two pounds on the plea that he had become married at the beginning of the week to a publican's daughter at Oldham."

"Did you send it?" asked Erb, with great cheerfulness.

"I wrote and I told him that if, as he said, he had in the past lent me sums amounting in the aggregate to this total, why I could only say that the fact had escaped my memory. I would, however, take an opportunity of looking through my memoranda in order to see whether I had made any record of such transactions. Could I say anything fairer?"

"And he's actually married?"

"There is a piece of what is termed wedding cake at home, awaiting my daughter's return."

"Will it—will it upset her do you think?" asked Erb nervously.

"I shall warn her not to eat it," said the Professor.

Erb did an extraordinary thing. Delighted by the news which the Professor had brought he set out upon a walk down through Camberwell into Surrey, a walk that he determined should last until he was tired out, a walk that had some vague advantage of going in the direction of Worthing. He was not used to heroic physical exercise, but on this unique occasion there seemed nothing else to do that would have been appropriate, and he mingled with the evening tide of people receding from London, beating it easily, and finally arriving beyond Dulwich, and well out into the country, where the rare gas lamps were being lighted and a mist came like a decorous veil and protected the face of the roadway modestly. Easier to think here than in the hurry and turmoil and clatter of town. After all, what did public life matter, what did the cause of labour or anything else matter so long as one was personally happy? That had ever been the aim of wise men; in future it should be his. There could always come the superadded amusement of playing with lesser minds, directing them and making them perform, exercising control in the manner of the unseen director of a Punch and Judy show. Erb argued this in a quiet road, with gesture and excitement; a sparrow hopped along for some distance with him in a companionable way, twittering approval, and hinting that if there should be such a thing in the corner of a pocket as a few bread crumbs—

It was late when Erb returned by train from Croydon to South Bermondsey station, and in the nearly empty rooms of Page's Walk he found Payne awaiting him. Payne, with something more than his usual gravity of countenance, seated on the one remaining chair and smoking an empty pipe in a desolate, absent minded way.

"Well," said Payne lugubriously, "you've done for yourself now."

"That so," remarked Erb. "What's the latest?"

"One of the worst crisisises," said Payne solemnly, and taking some gloomy enjoyment in making the word as long and as important as possible, "that ever you encountered in all your puff."

"I'm ready for it," said Erb.

"They've sacked you," said Payne.

"Is that all?"

"They've shown you the door. They've helped you downstairs with their foot. They've kicked you out, old man."

"This a joke?" asked Erb.

"Never made a joke in me life," declared Payne, "and well you know it."

Erb went over to the window and rested on the window sill.

"Spanswick?" he asked briefly.

"Him," answered Payne, "and no other."

"And they settled it all without hearing my account of the case?"

"Old chum! there didn't seem to be no room for any other account. He'd got chapter and verse for everything he said. All about a twenty pound cheque, all about—"

"And it never occurred to this—this flock of sheep," shouted Erb excitedly, "that I destroyed that cheque and never cashed it?"

"I don't think they understand much about cheques," said Payne. "The fact that you took it was what impressed them."

Neither spoke for a few minutes.

"Who's going to take my place?"

"Friend of Spanswick's."

"Name Doubleday?"

"Name of Doubleday," said Payne affirmatively. "Clever sort of sweat, so far as I could judge. What are you going to do about it, old man? Going to organise, I trust. Open air meeting, say."

"Did any of the others stick up for my side?"

"Only me!"

A pause again.

"Well, you're going to do something?"

"You've got another guess," said Erb.

CHAPTER XV

If Erb's experience of life had been greater, if his knowledge of the trend of events had been more extensive, he would have been helped by the assurance that in this world, mist and sunshine alternate, and that rarely a fog descends on the life of an energetic man and remains there always. But had Erb known this, there would still have remained the undeniable fact that, for the time at any rate, the atmosphere was murky. He showed a certain amount of temper. He sent in his keys addressed to the acting secretary, and, knowing that the accounts were all in order, declined the request that he should attend to explain money matters to his successor; he decided to leave London (having indeed very little there to leave) and to go down to Worthing, giving no one but Payne his address.

"Looks as though you had turned sulky," remonstrated Payne.

"I have!" said Erb.

The new number of "The Carman," which he himself had made up, contained a brief paragraph, to make room for which a quotation from Ruskin had been deleted.

"We beg to state that Herbert Barnes has no longer any connection with the Society, and that the position of Secretary will be filled up at the next meeting of the committee. At present everything points to Friend Doubleday, who is in a position to devote the whole of his time to the work, and can be relied on not to have dealings with the representatives of capital."

More stings came on the way up the Boro' to London Bridge station. Four railway carmen he met, driving their vans, instead of the "Hello!" and the mystic twist of the whip, there was first a glance of cautious recognition, then a steady look ahead, with an air of absorbed interest, as though realising for the first time the horse's presence. At the station itself, men of his old Society, on seeing him, hurried round to the tails of their vans, and commenced sorting parcels there with amazing industry. All this sent Erb into the deeper depths, and it was not until he reached Worthing, and found on the platform Rosalind and Aunt Emma and his sister, Louisa, Louisa's white face becoming pink with excitement, that he forgot his worries.

"Well," said Aunt Emma, "what's the best news?"

"There isn't any best news," replied Erb.

They went, arm in arm, down the long road to the sea front, and in a shelter there, Erb sat between them, and for the first time since the downfall found the luxury of detailed description and frank avowal. When the account came of the worst Rosalind touched his sleeve sympathetically.

"And there you are!" said Erb when he had finished. He found himself now inclined to look on the disasters as though they had occurred to someone else with whom he had nothing in common. "And here I am, in about as awkward a situation as I've ever been in in all my life."

"Complimentary to us," said Rosalind brightly.

He took her hand and patted it.

"You know what I mean," he whispered.

"They'd no right to sell up the 'ome," said Louisa fiercely.

"Yes they had," said Erb. "By the law."

"But that Spanswick's the one that should have suffered."

"An oven in a oast house," suggested Aunt Emma, "would finish him off. That's how he'll be treated in the next world, anyway."

"I ought to have verified the information he gave me about the first affair."

"And in the second affair you were perfectly right."

"That don't make any difference to the law of libel. Besides, I was in a temper when I wrote it. I let my feelings get the better of me."

"What do you propose—"

"Haven't a single idea," declared Erb exultantly. "Go back on me hands and knees and get a berth as carman again, I s'pose."

"That you never shall," said the two young women emphatically. "You have some long walks whilst you're down here," counselled Rosalind, "and think it over by yourself."

"If a bit of money's wanted—" began Aunt Emma.

"All this time," he said, turning to Louisa and pinching her white cheek, "all this time I haven't inquired how you are pulling along."

"I'm as right as rain, Erb."

"Ah!" he remarked doubtfully, "so you've always said. Heard anything of Alice?"

"Not a word from the overgrown minx," said Louisa with wrath. "If she was here I'd speak my mind to her, and pretty quick about it, too. Oh, yes, I know," Louisa went on, not to be deterred by an interruption from the rare luxury of an access of temper, "she may have a lot to think of; she takes jolly good care not to think of us."

"Has anyone written to tell her?" asked Rosalind quietly.

"Why should we?" demanded Erb's young sister with illogical heat. "It's her business to find out! But, of course, she wouldn't care if we was both in the workhouse."

"I wouldn't go so far as that."

"I shouldn't let you," said Aunt Emma.

"Meanwhile," interrupted Rosalind, "we're not giving your brother anything to eat. Let me run off to our rooms and get something ready."

The opportunity came here for Louisa to tell her brother how good Rosalind had been, what a first class nurse she had proved herself, how bright and attentive. "I should have kicked the bucket, I think," said Louisa looking out across the sea rather thoughtfully, "if it hadn't been for her. And such a manager! Isn't she, Aunt Emma?" Erb listening, began to feel that the world was not such a bad world after all. He talked hopefully, but vaguely, of either going to Canada, where he believed a man with a handful of capital was welcomed, and estates presented to him by a hospitable Government, or to New South Wales, where, so far as he could ascertain, labour leaders were in demand, and treated with proper amount of trustfulness. On Aunt Emma asking whether these places were not in point of fact a long way off, Erb was forced to admit that they were a pretty tidy step, and that, everything else being equal, he would prefer to stay in the London where he had been born—the London that he knew, the London that he liked.

"I haven't played the game well," admitted Erb candidly. "I've tried to be fair and straightforward with both sides, and I've managed to fall down in between them. And I've hurt myself!"

They had nearly finished their steak at dinner, and Louisa, breaking from new and fiercer condemnation of Alice, was about to inquire of Rosalind whether there was anything for after, when a miniature telegraph boy passed the window in Portland Street, and gave a double knock, altogether out of proportion to his size, at the front door. The landlady's daughter brought in a telegram, and "Please," said the landlady's daughter (inspecting Erb with curiosity, in order to give a report to her mother), "Please is there any answer?"

"Just heard of trouble. Lady Frances wishes to see you this evening. Most important.—ALICE."

"Take no notice of it," said Louisa, not yet restored to coolness. "Ignore it!"

Rosalind offered no counsel. Aunt Emma watched her narrowly. Erb considered for a moment, looking from one to another.

"Thought you were going to stay with us a few days?" remarked his sister.

"I ought to go back if it's really important," he said. "And Lady Frances is a young lady who doesn't like being disappointed."

"Please yourself," said Aunt Emma shortly. "But take care, that's all!"

He found news, on his return after this very brief visit, in a letter at the emptied rooms in Page's Walk that at once encouraged him and gave him perturbation. The white haired Labour Member wrote in cautious terms that a certain bye election in a London constituency was imminent. It had been decided to run a Labour candidate; the other two sides were pretty evenly matched, and if the game were played well, and played out, there was good chance of the Labour man making a fair show; there was another chance, less probable, but possible, that the Liberal candidate, if he found he had no prospect of winning, might retire before the election. The point was (wrote the Labour M.P.), would Erb consent to stand if he were selected? All the expenses would be paid, and all the help that the party could give would be willingly afforded. It would be better to put up a man like Erb, who had never before submitted to the suffrages of a constituency, than a man who had elsewhere undergone the experience of rejection. A reply to the House of Commons would oblige, and, meanwhile, this communication was to be regarded as strictly private.

"He hasn't heard," said Erb thoughtfully, "of my come down."

There were many courses, Erb felt, to pursue which were not straightforward, but only one that was honest. He went into a stationer's in Willow Walk, and, borrowing pen and ink, and purchasing paper and envelope, wrote a frank letter, giving all the necessary details of recent events, and just caught the five thirty post as the pillar box was being deprived of its contents. Then he made his way on foot—a desperate spirit of economy possessing him—to Eaton Square.

"Ages since I saw you," said Mr. Danks the footman, receiving him on the area steps with something like enthusiasm, "but I've heard of you over and over again."

"How are you getting on with your aitches?" asked Erb.

"Very complimentary remarks, too," said Mr. Danks, ignoring the inquiry. "My cousin Rosie seems to think of nobody else, so far as I can judge. I'd no idea you were a favourite with the fair sex!"

"Ah!" remarked Erb. "It's brain that tells in the long run."

"If I thought there was anything in that remark," said the footman, interested, "I'd go in for literature or something of the kind myself. I'm expecting to be thrown over by a young lady in Lowndes Square by every post, and—but I'm keeping you waiting."

"I noticed that," said Erb.

"Jackson," said cook, now stouter and apparently shorter than ever, "would be down directly." Would Erb let her cut for him a sandwich or a snack of—well, Erb could please himself, cook's own motto in the matter of feeding was, "Little and often," but it had never been her way to force her opinions on other people, in which particular her motto was "Interfere with nobody, and nobody will interfere with you." Cook had many other aphorisms to impart, and seemed a little hurt when Alice came into the kitchen and claimed her brother with a kiss that had about it unexpected affection.

"I've been worrying about you day and night," declared Alice. "I never thought anything would upset me so much."

"Wonder you don't ask after Jessie," interrupted cook.

"Jessie who?" demanded Erb.

"Just Jessie! Thought you was rather struck on her. She's with a family travelling abroad now. Tall girl with eyes."

"I'd forgotten all about her."

"Ah!" sighed the cook. "That's a man all over. It's the old saying over again—"

"And I told Lady Frances," continued Alice, leaving cook to mutter to a large joint of beef turning before a desperately fierce fire, "and you're to see her, Erb, directly after dinner."

"What's in the wind?"

"That's more than I can tell you. But I'm very glad you've cut your connection with all those common working men."

"They've cut their connection with me," said Erb.

"Comes to the same thing," said his sister, equably.

"Last time you was here, Mr. Barnes," said cook, over her shoulder from the fire, "you came as a friend of the family. Funny world isn't it? Upstairs one day, downstairs the next."

"You must be short of money, Erb," whispered his sister, in an undertone. "I've got quite a tidy bit put away in the savings bank. If ten or twenty pounds—"

"Upon my word," cried Erb, "it's worth while having a touch of misfortune now and again, if it's only just to find how much kindness there is about. But I shall find my feet somehow, Alice. Don't you worry about me."

"Can't help doing so."

"You might do what you can for Louisa, though. If it hadn't been for—for a friend of mine, I don't know where she'd have been."

"We've never quite got on together in the past," said Alice regretfully. "The difference in our heights seem to have led to other differences. But I'll see that it all dries straight. She'll pull through, of course."

"I think she'll just pull through," said Erb, thoughtfully, "and that's about all. Doctor says that if there was unlimited money about she'd be herself in a few months. But there you are, you see! Just when it's wanted particularly, it goes and hides."

Mr. Danks knocked and came in with a reverential air that differed from the one with which he had greeted Erb in the area. Lady Frances' compliments, and she would be pleased to see Mr. Barnes in the drawing room now.

"Let me put your tie straight," said Alice.

Lady Frances, looking taller and more charming than ever in her dinner dress, was delighted to see Mr. Barnes again. Quite a long time since they had met. She herself had been very busy—would not Mr. Barnes sit down?—very busy, and that must be taken as her excuse, rather worried, too. There was trouble out in North Africa, and when one had friends there—But the point was this: Lady Frances had heard all about the disastrous events in the Barnes household. In regard to Louisa, she must go to the Riviera with Lady Frances this winter. No, no! It was entirely a selfish proposition, and Louisa would be a most amusing companion; Lady Frances never tired of Cockney humour.

"In return for which," said Erb, fervently, "I'll do any blessed thing you like to ask me."

"So far, good!" said Lady Frances, with a gesture of applause with her fan. "Now to get on a little further. Her uncle—Mr. Barnes remembered her uncle?"

"I remember him well!"

"Now, this was a great secret, and must not be mentioned to a soul. Her uncle was going to stand for the coming bye election at—Ah! Mr. Barnes had heard of the probable vacancy. Strange how information flew about—and in this constituency" (here Lady Frances tried to wrinkle her smooth young forehead, and to look extremely wise), "there was, it appeared, a large working class element. Mr. Barnes had been useful in a somewhat similar way before. Why should not he again be of assistance? The money that he would thus earn would enable him to do almost anything. Go abroad to one of the Colonies, or stay here and marry and settle down, or—"

"There's just this about it that I ought to tell you," said Erb. "I've been asked to have a dash at the same event as an Independent Labour Candidate."

That, Lady Frances admitted with another effort to look aged, that certainly did complicate matters. Was there probability of Mr. Barnes accepting the offer?

"Not the least probability in the world."

Capital, capital! The young diplomatist again signified approval with her fan and leaned forward from her chair in a most attractive way. All that now remained to do was for Mr. Barnes to say "yes," and the whole matter would be arranged satisfactorily.

"Upon my word," declared Erb, after a few moments' thought, "to say 'yes' would be far and away the easiest thing to do. I owe precious little to my men after the way they've treated me, and it would just let them see—"

Mr. Barnes would excuse Lady Frances for interrupting, but a really most supremely brilliant idea had just occurred to her, and it was indispensable that she should communicate it without an instant's delay. (The young woman panted with surprise and enthusiasm, and Erb watched her reverently.) Why should not Mr. Barnes—this was absolutely the greatest notion that had ever occurred to anybody since the world began—why should not Mr. Barnes do everything he could to forward his candidature as an Independent, and then, just at the last moment retire in favour of—

"No!" said Erb suddenly.

The young woman did not conceal her disappointment at Erb's unreasonable attitude. No ambassador rebuffed in a mission on which future promotion depended, could have felt greater annoyance. But she recovered her usual amiability, and, leaving the discussion where it was, spoke further of her intentions in regard to Louisa and the trip to the South of France, on which subject she showed such real kindness that when Erb was presently shown out into Eaton Square by Mr. Danks ("Good evening, sir," said Mr. Danks respectfully), he felt something like contempt for himself for having declined so abruptly to accept her suggestion and advice. He went off to Payne's house, where something was done to a magic piece of furniture that pretended ordinarily to be a chair, whereupon it became a bedstead, and afforded comfortable rest for the night.

The next morning Erb, for about the first time in his life, found himself with nothing to do but to count the hours. He envied the easy carelessness of men able to loaf outside the public houses in Dover Street; in some public gardens near there were able bodied youths smoking cigarettes and sunning themselves luxuriously, content apparently to feel that there, at any rate, work could never force itself upon their attention, and no danger existed of encountering a job. Whatever happened, Erb knew that he would never slide down to this. It might well be that he would not find himself now in a position to ask Rosalind to become his wife, but he would never become a loafer. He walked up through the increasingly busy crowd of High Street, Borough, and comparison between their state and his forced him to recognise the fact that in no place, under certain conditions, can one be so lonely as in London.

"The very man!" cried a voice. The hook of a walking stick caught his arm.

"That you?" said Erb. "Get my letter?"

"Got your letter," said the white haired Labour M.P. in his swift, energetic way, "and I'm going down now to put everything straight for you."

"That'll take a bit of doing."

"I've had more twisted things to deal with than this. Which way were you going?"

"I scarcely know."

"Then you're coming down with me."

"Shan't I be rather in the way?"

"I hope so," said the Labour M.P.

A swift walker, the Labour M.P., and one with whom it was not easy to keep pace; he talked at a corresponding rate, so that by the time they reached the office of the London Railway Carmen's Society, he was showing signs of exhaustion, and the duty of talking to Spanswick, who was perched on the window sill on the landing, devolved upon Erb. Spanswick wore a look of perturbation and showed some desire not to look at Erb in speaking to him; he puffed at a ragged cigar, at which he glanced now and again with deep regret.

"I can't make 'ead or tail of it," said Spanswick, despondently. "It's a mystery, that's what it is. Why I should have trusted that man with untold gold."

"What's happened?" asked Erb.

"After all I've done for him, too," went on Spanswick. "I've treated him like a brother, I have; I might go so far as to say I've treated him more like a friend than a brother. It was only last night that we were 'aving a few friendly glasses together—I paid for the last, worse luck!—and he was talking about what he was going to do for the Society, and all the time he must have had this letter in his pocket, ready to pop in the post."

"Where's the key to this door?" asked the Labour M.P. sharply.

"He might well call himself Mister Doubleday," went on Spanswick, finding the key in his pocket, "I've never been more deceived in anybody in all my life. Him and me has been pals for over six weeks, and this is how he turns round and treats me."

"What on earth are you talking about?"

"I've seen him home when it's been necessary after the places were closed, and sometimes," Spanswick admitted this grudgingly, "sometimes of course, he's seen me 'ome when it's been necessary. He's told me things about his early boyhood; I've told him things about my early boyhood. If I've had more tobacco in me pouch than he has, he's always been welcome to a pipeful. I got him the best berth he ever had in all his born days—"

"And outed me from it," remarked Erb. "What—?"

"But don't it jest shew you," demanded Spanswick eagerly, "how the very best of us can sometimes be taken in? I'm looked on as a man who knows enough to come in when it rains, and I certainly pride myself more on taking in others than being took in meself. And here am I, in me fortysecond year—"

"Barnes!" called the voice of the Labour M.P. from the office, "come here!"

Spanswick went on growling to himself as Erb left him and entered the office.

"The books do not appear to have been touched since you left," said the white haired man. "Not a figure, not a letter."

"Then he can't be accused of tampering with 'em."

"How much cash did you leave in the safe?" Erb showed the sum at the foot of a page in the accounts book. "I've half a mind," said the Labour M.P., in a determined way, that suggested he was making an understatement, "I have half a mind to break it open!"

"Wouldn't it be better to give him a chance of coming back?"

"Read that letter!"

Erb read a slip of paper that Doubleday had left on the desk. Doubleday had addressed it to the committee, and it told them that, finding his health was giving way under the stress of the few days' work, he had decided to take a holiday. If there should be any little trifle short in the cash accounts, that would be replaced as soon as he could make it convenient to do so. He added that he had drawn the sum standing to the Society's credit, because there was not enough money in the safe to enable him to take the somewhat lengthened holiday which he felt was necessary. Thanking them for all past favours, regretting their acquaintance had been so brief, and wishing the Society every success, he remained, Theirs faithfully, Edward H. Doubleday.

"I'd like to know the worst," said the Labour M.P. "I suppose you've no experience in forcing looks?"

"It's a branch of my education," replied Erb, "that's been sadly neg—Why, the blessed thing's open!"

The safe was, indeed, unlocked, and this mattered the less, because the safe was quite empty. Erb struck a match and searched the corners; there was nothing to be seen but an envelope bearing the words, "I.O.U.," a certain large amount, and Doubleday's portentous signature.

"What's the next step, sir?" asked Erb.

"Set the police on his track."

"And the next?"

"Call the committee together at the earliest possible moment. Make them do what I should have induced them to do even though this had not happened—reinstate you as secretary."

"Anything else?"

"After that you and I can talk over this bye election business. I think we shall get you in the House, Barnes, before you're very much older." The M.P. looked at his large silver watch, "I must be moving. Deputation to the Home Secretary at one. Fine life ours, Barnes; always something doing. Always difficulties to be cleared away. You'll enjoy it when you're in the midst of it."

"Think so?"

The Labour M.P. hurried off, pushing Spanswick aside as that desolate man made an effort to impart some further details of his acute grievance. Spanswick went to the door of the office, but found it shut in his face.

"Now, if I'd been in his place," cried Spanswick, through the keyhole, "the least I should have thought of saying would have been "Alves!'"

CHAPTER XVI

The bustle, the hurry, the excitement were again here; the grievance that a day contained, only twenty four hours reconstituted itself; the feeling came once more that one was a person of some importance. But Erb, spite the old environments, found himself wanting in enthusiasm. He could not deny this, although for a time he tried to do so. Face to face with a situation that a month earlier would have aroused all his most aggressive instincts, he found he was quite unable to feel any excitement in the matter. The rebuff the men had given him he could not forget; the empty space that the dispute had made could not be easily bridged. Moreover, there were other matters which seemed larger and much more important than this to occupy his consideration. Rosalind brought Louisa back to town, the vacation being over, and Camberwell desiring to go on with its lessons in voice production, and Lady Frances, hearing of this from Alice, antedated her trip to the Continent, and, in her generous way, prepared to fly off with Louisa and Jessie, the maid; Louisa, dazed by the rapidity of events, said goodbye with apparent calm to her brother and her three most recent fiancés.

"Likely as not," said Louisa casually, "I shall marry one of you when I come back!"

"Which?" inquired the three youths eagerly.

"The one that's got the most money."

"Ah!" said the young baker from Rotherhithe New Road contentedly.

"And the most sense."

"Good!" remarked the assistant from the Free Library.

"And the best temper."

"Right o!" said the booking clerk from Walworth Road station.

Lady Frances asked Erb to get an evening paper, and he went to the small bookstall on the platform. The train was on the point of starting, and he took up a Conservative evening paper. As he did so, he glanced at the placard that was being pinned to the stall, and observed a line "Massacre of English Commission in Morocco." He quickly bought another journal of an earlier edition. Later, when the train had gone, he found in the "fudge" of the first journal a brief message, printed unevenly, with a similar heading:—

"The Foreign Office has received news of the massacre of the English Commission recently sent out to Morocco. No particulars are to hand, but the Commission included the Lieutenant the Hon.—"

"Her young man!" cried Erb distressedly. "Thought as much! This'll be a fearful upset for her."

He had some idea of going at once to Eaton Square, but this seemed of little use, and he had become so much accustomed to consulting Rosalind that he decided instead to go down to Southampton Street. Arrived there, he found commotion of such importance that this trouble concerning Lady Frances took a second place.

An ambulance stood inside the gate, near to the specimens of graveyard statuary, and on the steps of the house, a constable.

"Are you," asks C 243, barring the way, "any relation to the deceased? By deceased," explains the constable, giving additional information with great wariness, "he doesn't, of course, mean deceased exactly, but nearly as good as that; he means old gentleman—white haired old gentleman—that was knocked down by a cab in the Strand not half an hour ago, as he stooped down in the middle of the roadway to pick up a halfpenny he dropped. Happened just at the corner of Wellington Street, it did. Knew the old chap by sight. One of what C 243 ventures to call the regulars. See them every day between Bedford Street and Wellington Street. You don't know their names, of course," says constable argumentatively, "but, bless your soul, you know their faces so well that, when one of them drops out, it makes you feel as though you've lost a personal friend. Every one of them on the cadge, so C 243 understands, and apparently manage to live on by borrowing from each other. A rum life, if ever there was one; no two ways about that."

"Is he still able to recognise—?"

"Old chap's first words were 'Not a hospital; take me home.' Constable inquired where was home, and old chap managed to give the address. Whereupon constable, after deliberation with a colleague, decided to take four wheeler and see old chap home as desired. Thought, perhaps, he was only a bit stunned. Or, perhaps, dazed. Instead of which, coming past the Obelisk, old chap suddenly lurched forward, and—"

The small servant came out and beckoned. The voice of Rosalind called gently.

"I am here," replies Erb.

"Want you just one moment."

A boy doctor who stood inside the room, endeavouring to wear a look of uncountable years, nodded curtly, and went to the foot of the sofa. On the sofa lay the Professor, with a rug thrown over him, the rug close up to his chin, one hand free, and travelling restlessly over the pattern.

"That bourne," whispered the Professor, "from which no traveller—You are a good lad, and you will look after her."

"If she'll let me," says Erb. "How are you feeling, sir, by this time?"

"Look after her better than I have done. See that when you arrive at my state, laddie, you—you can glance back on your life with content."

Erb, with a kindly touch, pushed the Professor's hair from his eyes, and the old man looked up gratefully. Erb touched his hand, and the hand gripped his as though with desire to attach itself to something reliable.

"I'm slipping," said the Professor simply. He closed his eyes, and presently reopened them as with difficulty. "We few, we happy few, we band of brothers. Give me the word, sir, give me the word. What in Heaven's name," with sudden indignation, "is the use of having a prompter if—"

Rosalind, keeping her tears back, came with the heavy volume, opening it quickly at the place where a ringletted youth in a steel engraving was addressing soldiers.

Erb discovering the lines with the aid of Rosalind's finger, gave the cue. "For he to day—" The old Professor goes on.

"'For he to day that sheds his blood with me Shall be my be rother! be he ne'er so vile, This day shall gentle his condition, And gentlemen in England, And gentlemen in England.' No use," said the Professor weakly, "my study's gone."

"Don't bother about it, sir."

"Laddie," said the Professor, "you—you think me a thriftless, miserable wastrel."

"No, no," answered Erb. "Not that exactly. But we're none of us perfect."

"I've reached me last hour, and the time has come for plain speech. I've been—" a smile dared to creep halfway across the Professor's face. "I've been a fraud."

"Father," said Rosalind brokenly. "You've always been the dearest, dearest—"

The boy doctor, snatching the opportunity to whisper to Erb, who could not lose the Professor's hand, said that he had administered a sleeping draught: if the Professor desired to say anything it would be better to allow him to speak without interruption.

"I have been a fraud," repeated the Professor, with something of relish. "I have been a—'Neither a borrower or a lender be. For borrowing oft—'"

"You've always been welcome, sir."

"I have been the most fraudulent of all frauds. There is a note in my desk to send to the 'Era.' I have often, in my salad days, advertised in the 'Era.' I think they will put it in."

"I'll pay them to, if necessary."

The Professor gave a faint echo of a chuckle. "How they will talk about it in the Strand! I'd give the remainder of my life to hear them."

The old, old mouth, twisted in the effort to display amusement, and remained twisted; one eyelid nearly closed. The boy doctor looked anxiously from the foot of the sofa: Rosalind knelt.

"You're going to have a nice long sleep, sir," said Erb, bending down. "And you'll wake up a different man, bless you."

"I shall wake up," repeated the Professor slowly, "wake up a different man."

Both eyelids closing now, he turned his white head a little towards the wall. Presently his grip of Erb's hand relaxed, and Erb, disengaging himself, went with the others to the window, where the three spoke in an undertone, Erb holding Rosalind's elbows supportingly. A slight groan from the sofa called the doctor.

"All over," announced the boy doctor, with a desperate effort to assume the air of one used to making such announcements, and rendered callous by long centuries of habit. "I'll let the Coroner's officer know. Don't mind my running off, do you? Fearfully busy, just now."

The Professor's words were counted as the mere wandering of speech, and dismissed from memory until, when the inquest was over, and some days later the journey to Honor Oak cemetery and back at an end, Erb took upon himself the duty of examining the locked drawers of the desk. Then it was found that tardily in his life, the Professor had hinted at truth, for books entitled Post Office Savings Bank were discovered there, and it was realised that this old spendthrift, this most careless member of a careless profession, had hoarded carefully throughout his life, engaging stray half crowns, only to add them instantly to his store, and the five brown covered books announced that to his credit stood what seemed to Erb and to Rosalind the extravagant fortune of nearly four hundred pounds. A will, drawn up in commendable order, directed that all this was left to "my dear daughter Rosalind, and may she forgive her father for many shortcomings, and think of him if she can, with affection and regard."

"This," said Erb, when he had reckoned up the amounts on a slip of paper, "this is very satisfactory for you, but it makes all the difference to me."

"It's going to make no sort of difference whatever," said Rosalind emphatically.

"Money matters always do."

"Depends on the people who have the money. Money in itself doesn't bring happiness, but it doesn't follow that it destroys it. Your Lady Frances, for instance—"

"What makes you call her my Lady Frances?"

"She looks upon you as her property," said Rosalind, turning away.

"If I hadn't got such a stiff collar on I'd laugh," declared Erb. "By the bye, I'm very glad to see by to day's papers that her sweetheart was on his way back before that nasty affair took place out near Tetuan; mysterious thing, rather. Been telegraphed for apparently, by somebody."

"I know."

"You saw about it in the paper?"

"No," said Rosalind.

"Well, but how—"

"I sent the telegram," she said quietly. "I thought it better he should be back here. I didn't want her to get you."

Erb took her hands. She tried to keep her lips from his, but she tried for a moment only.

"This simplifies matters," he said. "I never could tell whether you liked me or not."

"You never asked!"

"People will say I married you for your money," he said half jokingly.

"And I shall know," replied Rosalind, patting his face, "that you married me because—because you liked me."

CHAPTER XVII

Silk hatted men were hurrying to and fro in the lobby, each with an air of bearing the responsibilities of the Empire on his shoulders; cards were being sent in by the attendants: a few country visitors stood about near to the statue of Mr. Gladstone waiting awkwardly for the arrival of their member. Swing doors moved unceasingly: now and again two members would encounter each other and consult furtively with wrinkled foreheads, and visitors stood back from the round space at the centre with awe and respect, giving them room. Erb, in a morning coat and a necktie of such gaiety, that alone it betrayed the fact of his wedding day, was an event not yet forgotten, strolled about, less appalled by the surroundings than most, so that provincials came to him now and again and made inquiries. Whenever he had been to the House before he had always felt wistful, and had looked through corridor to the inner lobby with anticipation; this evening the feeling was absent.

"Haven't kept you waiting I hope, Barnes?" The white haired Labour member bustling out was conspicuous by reason of his bowler hat. "Rather a lot of things to do one way and another. When you get here you'll find—I can't see him now," answering a messenger. "Tell him I'm going down to Bermondsey to put something straight that has got crooked, and I shall not be back till ten. Tell him that!"

"Cab or 'bus?" inquired Erb, as they went down the broad steps.

"'Bus," said the Labour member, promptly. "Somebody might see us if we took a hansom. You'll find that you can't be too careful. And there's another thing, too. Flower in your coat, you know—"

With axiom and words of counsel, the white haired member shortened the journey from Westminster to the rooms in Grange Road; Erb listening with a proper deference, and refraining from all but appropriate and well chosen interruptions. The member appeared stimulated by the task before him, and Erb felt quite mature in remembering the time when he, too, would have found his blood run quicker at the prospect of argument. His companion hurried up the corkscrew staircase of the coffee house, Erb following slowly, nodding to a few of the men who, with anxious expression of countenance stood about on the landing. He went into a room at the side, where he hoped to be alone. Spanswick, however, had seen him, and Spanswick, following in, took a wooden chair on the opposite side of the table. But Erb's old van boy interposed, big with a message. The chief had sent him (said William Henry) to mention in confidence that, if Erb cared to come back to his former position—"Extraordinary thing," said Erb, "how much the world wants you when you show that you don't want the world. No answer, William Henry, only thanks."

"I've been telling a lot of 'em," said Spanswick, jerking his hand in the direction of the other room as the young diplomatist went, "that if they take my advice, Erb, they'll ask you to come back."

"I see!"

"I've pointed out to 'em that they've blundered all along. That matter of the cheque, for instance—it's proved that it's never been cashed and, therefore, as I say, the money could never have come into your pocket. On the top of that," said Spanswick, with something like indignation, "they go and select a bounder like old Doubleday. Why I could see what the man was like from the very start. I took his measure the first time I came across him. A talkative, interfering, muddle headed gas bag—I told some of 'em that it was a wonder they got men to take the trouble to lead them at all."

"It is a wonder!"

"And here they are now," said Spanswick, rising to go and join in the deliberations of the next room, "here they are now down on their 'ands and knees without a single penny in the cash box, worse off than they've ever been ever since the Society started, and not one amongst 'em capable of taking what you may call the reins of government in hand. It all comes," concluded Spanswick, tapping at his nose with his forefinger, "it all comes through people not listening to the advice of the few of us," here he struck his waistcoat impressively, "the few of us, either me and you, that know."

Through the partition Erb could hear the voice of the Labour member. Impossible to distinguish the words, but clearly there was reproof in the tones at first; this gave place later to the quieter key of counsel. The men who had hitherto been silent began to applaud; fists struck the table with approval, and presently there came the sound of emphatic cheering that had often made Erb warm with pleasure.

"You're wanted, old man," said Payne, opening the door importantly. "Foller me into the next room, will you?"

The old scent of gas and cheap tobacco and corduroys. The old faces looking round as he entered, elbows resting on the table, some of the men with tumblers before them, others, wearing the stern look of sobriety, had been making notes of the speech to which they had just listened. Circular stains on the long wooden T shaped tables; the impaled advertisements on the wall awry as though affected by the perfumes coming up from the bar downstairs. The dulled mirrors at the end reflected the room mistily with its frame protected eternally by tissue paper. The barman waiting for orders at the doorway gave Erb a tap of encouragement as he went in.

"Bravo! vo! vo! vo!" murmured the room.

"Order! order!" said the Chairman. "I call on our old and trusted friend—I forget his blessed name—from Paddington Parcels, at any rate, to address the meeting."

The Paddington Parcels member cleared his throat and rose. He had been one of the first to go over, and this he frankly admitted. "Gives me all the more title," said Paddington Parcels determinedly, "to undertake what I'm undertaking of now."

Paddington Parcels handsomely offered to cut a long story short, and the room gave encouragement to this proposal, whereupon he proceeded to speak at intolerable length with ever, "Just one word and I've done," and "Let me add a couple of words more," and "Finally, I should like to remark," and other phrases all suggesting an immediate finish, anticipation not justified by results.

Summarised, the argument was that the society had made a grievous blunder; that when a chap made a mistake he should apologise for it and set it right; that a society was like a chap, and should behave as a chap would, and that in the present deplorable state of the society there was only one thing they could do, namely, to ask Erb Barnes to let byegones be byegones, and to come back and resume the secretaryship. When, after many feints of sitting down, thus arousing the oratorical desires of those anxious to second the resolution, and always thinking of more words that retained him in a standing position, Paddington Parcels did unexpectedly resume his seat, there was great competition for the honour of speaking next, and twenty faces looked gloomy and disappointed when Payne was selected. Payne spoke briefly. Every society had its ups and downs: this society was just now all in the downs, as the song had it. But it was well worth while to have such an experience, if only to see his old chum, his good old chum Erb, righted in the eyes of everybody and restored to a position that he ought never to have quitted.

The Labour member begged leave (his tones intimating nothing of humility) to say a few words before this was put to the vote. The society had been compared to a man, but the society, as a society, was, so to speak, a mere child, and it had recently behaved in the impulsive wrong headed manner of a child. That might be overlooked once; it would not be overlooked a second time. Mind that! Brains had been served out to one and all, but some hadn't quite got their proper share with the result that others had more than the average supply, and if the man who had come out rather short in the matter had not sufficient sense, when in a position of difficulty, to ask advice from those fully equipped, why the men with the short supply would have to put up with the consequences of their own blundering. And there was another thing. The success of the labour movement as a whole depended on the loyalty of the men to those who were doing brain work on their behalf; let that loyalty once exhibit anything of doubt and the whole scheme, the whole business, the whole movement—the Labour member struck the wooden table emphatically at each variant of the phrase—the whole show would go to pot. All the same, he congratulated them on the wise decision at which they were about to arrive, and he strongly urged his friend Erb Barnes, "in consideration of certain prospective events," said the white haired member, lowering his voice mysteriously, "of which he is aware, but cannot at the present time be made public," to accept good temperedly the invitation of the men.

The men had kept silent whilst receiving criticism; at these last words they rose from the Windsor chairs and shouted approval. The shirt sleeved waiter went up and down the tables, culling empty glasses and making them into a bouquet. Erb went to the mantelpiece, and resting one hand there, spoke quietly. Every face turned in his direction. "I think," said the Chairman importantly, "I think I may say carried per se—I mean nem. con."

"I'm not going to occupy your time for long," said Erb from the fireplace when the renewed cheering had ceased. "You'll have other business to do—(No, no)—and, contrary to my usual practice I'm going to be very brief indeed. There have been times when you've heard me speak at a considerable length, and for all your kindness to me under those circumstances I give you my thanks. I shan't ever trouble you again to that extent. A month or so ago you met here—you, just the same men that you are now—and you gave me the sack. You never gave me a chance of defending myself or explaining my actions; you just pushed me off."

The room murmured an unintelligible protest.

"You just pushed me off. You jilted me. You broke off the engagement. Chaps, that broken engagement can't be mended. We're all constituted differently, I suppose, but I'm like this: if anybody's faithful to me I should be glad of the opportunity of going through fire and water for them, if they're not, then fire and water are things they can go through for themselves. I reckon I've been in love with this society for the last year, and I've been loyal to it; now I'm in love with somebody else."

"Who?" demanded the room.

"I'm in love," said Erb, turning to glance at himself contentedly in the clouded mirror, "in love with my wife."

"In love with his wife!" said the members to each other amazedly.

"Some people possess a stock of enthusiasm that's got no limits; mine all vanished, I find, directly you treated me unfairly. My friend who's kindly come down from Westminster to talk to you knows that I'm giving up prospects that would tempt a good many; it's only honest to tell you that those prospects, which a month since would have made my head swell, at this moment don't allure me in the slightest degree. I think—I don't know, mind—I think I'm seeing things clearer than I did. I thought all the right and all the justice and all the everything was on our side; I've come to see that, as a matter of fact, it's about fairly divided. I'm going to take up a little business on my own account down in Wandsworth as a master carman, and I should be very glad, chaps, if you could manage to—to wish me luck. I'm going now. I'm going to leave you to go on with the business of appointing a secretary. There's plenty of capable men in the world, and the opportunity always finds them. So I wish you every prosperity, and I wish we may always keep friends, because some day we might find ourselves shoulder to shoulder again. And I wish you—" Erb hesitated for a moment in order to steady his voice, "I wish you good bye."

The men crowded towards the doorway as Erb went in that direction.

"Come back to us, old man," they cried. "We want you. Can't you see that—"

On the opposite side of the roadway below, warmly jacketed in view of the coolness of an autumn evening, a pleasant figure walked to and fro. Regardless of the circumstances that faces looked down from the windows, Erb hurried across and kissed her.

Up the street they walked, arm in arm with each other, and arm in arm with happiness.

William Pett Ridge – A Short Biography

William Pett Ridge was born at Chartham, near Canterbury, Kent, on 22nd April 1859.

His family's resources were certainly limited. His father was a railway porter, and the young Pett Ridge, after schooling in Marden, Kent became a clerk in a railway clearing-house. The hours were long and arduous, but self-improvement was Pett Ridge's goal. After working from nine until seven o'clock he would attend evening classes at Birkbeck Literary and Scientific Institute and then to follow his passion; the ambition to write. He was heavily influenced by Dickens and several critics thought he had the capability to be his successor.
From 1891 many of his humourous sketches were published in the St James's Gazette, the Idler, Windsor Magazine and other literary periodicals of the day.

Pett Ridge published his first novel in 1895, A Clever Wife. By the advent of his fifth novel, Mord Em'ly, a mere three years later in 1898, his success was obvious. His writing was written from the perspective of those born with no privilege and relied on his great talent to find humour and sympathy in his portrayal of working class life.

Today Pett Ridge and other East End novelists including Arthur Nevinson, Arthur Morrison and Edwin Pugh are being grouped together as the Cockney Novelists.

In 1924, Pugh set out his recollections of Pett Ridge from the 1890s: "I see him most clearly, as he was in those days, through a blue haze of tobacco smoke. We used sometimes to travel together from Waterloo to Worcester Park on our way to spend a Saturday afternoon and evening with H. G. Wells. Pett Ridge does not know it, but it was through watching him fill his pipe, as he sat opposite me in a stuffy little railway compartment, that I completed my own education as a smoker... Pett Ridge had a small, dark, rather spiky moustache in those days, and thick, dark, sleek hair which is perhaps not quite so thick or dark, though hardly less sleek nowadays than it was then".

With his success, on the back of his prolific output and commercial success, Pett Ridge gave generously of both time and money to charity. In 1907 he founded the Babies Home at Hoxton. This was one of several organisations that he supported that had the welfare of children as their mission.

His circle considered Pett Ridge to be one of life's natural bachelors. In 1909 They were rather surprised therefore when he married Olga Hentschel.

As the 1920's arrived Pett Ridge added to his popularity with the movies. Four of his books were adapted into films.

Pett Ridge now found the peak of his fame had passed. Although he still managed to produce a book a year he was falling out of fashion and favour with the reading public and his popularity declined rapidly. His canon runs to over sixty novels and short-story collections as well as many pieces for magazines and periodicals.

William Pett Ridge died, on 29th September 1930, at his home, Ampthill, Willow Grove, Chislehurst, at the age of 71.

He was cremated at West Norwood on 2nd October 1930.

William Pett Ridge – A Concise Bibliography

Minor Dialogues (1895)
A Clever Wife (1895)
An Important Man and Others (1896)
Second Opportunity of Mr Staplehurst (1896)
Mord Em'ly (1898)
Outside The Radius. Stories of a London suburb (1899)
A Son of the State (1899)
A Breaker of Laws (1900)
London Only. A Set Of Common Occurrences (1901)
Lost Property (1902)
Up Side Streets – Short Stories (1903)
Erb (1903)

George And The General (1904)
Next Door Neighbours (1904)
Mrs Galer's Business (1905)
The Wickhamses (1906)
Name of Garland (1907)
Speaking Rather Seriously (1908)
Sixty Nine Birnam Road (1908)
Table d'Hôte. Tales (1910)
Splendid Brother (1910)
From Nine to Six-Thirty (1910)
Light Refreshment (1911)
Thanks to Sanderson (1911)
Love at Paddington (1912)
Devoted Sparkes (1912)
The Remington Sentence (1913)
Mixed Grill (1913)
The Happy Recruit (1914)
The Kennedy People (1915)
Book Here – Short Stories (1915)
Stray Thoughts from W. Pett Ridge (1916)
Madam Prince (1916)
The Amazing Years (1917)
Special Performance (1918)
Well To Do Arthur (1920)
Just Open. Short Stories (1920)
Richard Triumphant (1922)
Lunch Basket – Tales (1923)
Miss Mannering (1923)
Rare Luck (1924)
Leaps And Bounds (1924)
A Story Teller – Forty Years In London (1923)
Just Like Aunt Bertha (1925)
I Like To Remember (1925)
Our Mr Willis (1926)
London Types Taken From Life (1926)
Easy Distances (1927)
The Two Mackenzies (1928)
The Slippery Ladder (1929)
Eldest Miss Collingwood (1930)
Led by Westmacott (1931)

William Pett Ridge also wrote a play titled "Four small plays"

www.ingramcontent.com/pod-product-compliance
Lightning Source LLC
Chambersburg PA
CBHW022118040426
42450CB00006B/751